Ernest Arthur Rowe

The life and work of a Victorian garden painter

DERRICK ROWE

Published by the author

First published in 2009

Edited and typeset by:
The Book of My Life
2nd Floor
145–157 St John Street
London
EC1V 4PY
0845 643 9423
www.bookofmylife.co.uk

Photography by Paul Anant LBIPP, LRPS
www.paulanant.com

ISBN: 978-0-9561411-0-1

Printed and bound in Great Britain by:
BAS Fine Art Printers
Unit 2b, Minton Distribution Park
London Road
Amesbury
Wiltshire
SP4 7RT

Dedication

For our grandchildren — Samantha, Owen, Bradley, Olivia, Harrison and Thomas

LIST OF ILLUSTRATIONS

The Long Border, Hampton Court .... front cover
Trinity Quad, Cambridge .... back cover
Ernest Arthur Rowe xi
Two lithographs 5
Formal Garden, Penshurst 7
The Royal Institute of Painters in Water Colours' President's medal 9
Two black and white portraits 10
The Old Dovecot 12
Evening Light 13
Clovelly Post Office 18
A Winter's Tale 20
Under the Apple Trees 21
The Pond in the Formal Garden, Penshurst 25
Sophy Slater and Ernest Arthur Rowe, Davos, 1895 29
Sophy Slater, 1896 29
Extract from a letter to Sophy, 1896 38
The Baptist Chapel, Bourton-on-the-Water 41
Arthur and Sophy, 1899 41
December on the Bay of Naples 47
The Church of the Madonna Della Grazia, Ravello 49
The Garden of the Cappuccini Monastery, Amalfi 51
View of Mount Etna from the Garden of St Domenico 52
Villa Carlotta, Tremezzo 54
Villa Buona Ventura, Cadenabbia 55
Extracts from a letter to Ronald Rowe 58

Charles V Pavilion, Alcazar, Seville 59
Coloured postcards sent by Ernest Arthur Rowe to his children in 1906 60–61
On the Banks of a Surrey Stream 66
Handwritten exhibition notice 68
Dean Hole's Garden, Rochester 73
The Long Border, Hampton Court 75
Photographs of Ravello, Arthur's house 76
Ravello 77
Blackhurst House 79
Extracts from letters sent from Levens Hall 82
Extracts from letters to Ronald Rowe, 1911 83
Photograph of Arthur, Sophy, Esmond, Mary, Ronald and Pip 85
Golders Hill Park 94
The North Front, Chequers Court 95
Vases and Peacocks 97
Trug of Roses 102

Introduction

"Not everyone sees beauty in a clipped yew hedge," so said Ernest Arthur Rowe in an interview with a writer from *The Girl's Realm (a monthly magazine for young gentlewomen)* in 1907, but it was Rowe's ability to see and reproduce the beauty in every corner of the gardens that he visited throughout his thirty-year career that made him so successful and earned him the patronage of Queen Mary and many other illustrious buyers of art.

Ernest Arthur Rowe was one of a small group of Victorian artists who specialised in painting the great formal gardens of England, Scotland and Ireland during the latter half of the nineteenth century. He captured in watercolours many famous gardens, including Abbey Leix, Berkeley Castle, Compton Wynyates and Hampton Court, at the height of summer when their clipped hedges were lush and verdant, and their borders were overflowing with blooms of vibrant colour. While the owners of these gardens strove for perfection on their canvasses of soil and stone, Rowe represented their vision with his considered employment of light and shade. In doing so he left lasting images of perfection — something that no gardener could ever hope to achieve.

Rowe was a great painter, but he was also shrewd with a

good understanding of what art collectors wanted. He realised that for many of the country's elite, gardening was a passion. They invested a huge amount of time and energy in creating extravagant and colourful outdoor spaces. Why would they not want to record their gardens in all their polychromatic glory? Helped by introductions from Christine Hamlyn, whom Rowe had met in Clovelly, North Devon, the artist began painting the gardens of many wealthy and influential people and sold numerous watercolours to the owners of the gardens in question. Along with the stately Clovelly Court, Mrs Hamlyn owned the entire village of Clovelly and its surrounding area, and many of her friends were equally prosperous. Aware of the importance of these people to his career, Rowe did not neglect to mention them, when interviewed for *The Girl's Realm* magazine, and their "kindness" in allowing him to paint their gardens. Whenever he held an exhibition he would seek the assistance of his wife, Sophy, and eldest son, Ronald, in sending out invitations to all the influential people whose names and addresses he had collected, and as a result of this enthusiasm and attention to detail his exhibitions were attended by numerous members of the aristocracy.

Passionate about painting in general, and his subject matter in particular, Rowe was utterly devoted to his work. Despite suffering the debilitating effects of tuberculosis for most of his life, he worked constantly. The summer months would be spent travelling between the grandest houses of Britain to paint their gardens. The winter months were almost invariably spent in his beloved Italy, where the artist would document many Italian gardens with his brush and paints while enjoying the benefits that the warm climate brought to his health. Rowe meticulously recorded all his travels in a notebook entitled *E.a.R's Book of Wanderings.* This unwavering commitment to his art resulted in a very large body of work. There are over six hundred paintings by Rowe listed in the Victoria and Albert Museum, which holds records of all the paintings that were exhibited during the period, and it is estimated that Rowe must have created over one thousand original works of art.

Although popular and successful during his lifetime Rowe had largely been forgotten after his death in 1922 until Christopher Wood, the foremost authority on Victorian artists, took an interest in Rowe's work. Wood's book *Painted Gardens: English Watercolours 1850–1914* (Pavilion Books) is devoted to the great Victorian painters of gardens including George Samuel Elgood,

Beatrice Parsons and Ernest Arthur Rowe. In his book, Wood praises Rowe's work and hails him as one of the masters of Victorian garden painting. "His watercolours," says Wood, "…give the impression that the sun was always shining."

In 1989 Queen Elizabeth II exhibited four of Rowe's paintings, originally purchased by Queen Mary, in an exhibition entitled *Royal Gardens of England* at Sandringham, and a new group of art lovers were made aware of his work.

The aim of this book is to introduce Ernest Arthur Rowe to a wider audience and to recognise him as a truly great garden painter, at least equal to any of his contemporaries, who has left behind a stunning body of work that accurately documents some of the grandest and loveliest gardens of the Victorian era. Hopefully the reproductions of his glorious paintings herein will speak for themselves.

Ernest Arthur Rowe
(1862–1922)

Chapter one

EARLY AMBITIONS

Ah, but a man's reach should exceed his grasp.
Or what's a heaven for?
Robert Browning

When writing to his future wife Sophy about his early life, in 1896, Ernest Arthur Rowe gave tantalisingly little information about the first sixteen years. Although he included a lot of detail about his experiences after that age, all he wrote about his childhood years was the following: "Born in 62 the youngest of 5…went to a middle class school until I was 16 years old (soon got through 16 years of my life)."

From the surviving records we know that Arthur, as he was known to his friends and family, was born on 21 August 1862 at Forest Lane, Stratford, Essex (now part of East London). His father, Thomas George Rowe, worked as a solicitor's clerk and as such was a member of the middle classes, which had been steadily increasing their numbers since the industrial revolution at the beginning of the century.[1] Thomas George was born in Maidstone and the family continued to have connections with the county of Kent, with the artist himself eventually settling in the area.

Growing up, Arthur had a good relationship with his mother Adelaide Rowe (née Wallis) and he remained close to her throughout her life. But Adelaide was deaf and it seems that she let her disability hold her back. In one letter to Sophy, Arthur commented that, "She has been the best of mothers to me but she has had no experience of the world, having been deaf since she was a young girl & never caring to go anywhere".

The family was a tightly knit one. When Arthur was older he supported, to varying degrees, his mother and elder sisters Florence Jane (Flo) and Adelaide Isabel (Bella). His eldest sister, Anne Elizabeth (Annie), frequently took care of Arthur's own children during their early years. It was only Arthur's one brother, George Henry, who appeared to escape his family responsibilities, leaving home once for a short stay in America and then for Tasmania where he managed a butter factory. George's flight inevitably had an impact on Arthur, who was then expected to shoulder much of the financial burden of his family members after the death of his father in 1885.

At some point during his childhood there may have been a downturn in the family's fortunes, as Arthur wrote in a letter to Sophy in 1896, "Don't think that we are at all grand in any way, we are of very humble origin and don't even keep a servant, haven't since I was five years old." It was common for middle-class families in the Victorian era to employ a maid. The Rowe family's loss of domestic help could have been caused by several factors. Perhaps there had been some loss of income that made keeping a servant no longer practical for the Rowes at this time. It may have been simply that the family moved house and there was no longer room for a maid. By the time Arthur was eight years old, census records show that the family was no longer living in Stratford but was by then at 14 Priory Road, Lambeth (now 129 Landsdowne Way).

The information on Arthur's boyhood is limited, but the little that is known, when pieced together, paints a picture of a fairly happy and carefree existence. Arthur's interest in old houses and gardens began as a child, perhaps on visits to relatives in Kent. According to an interview, "he would walk miles to see an old timber-house surrounded by some garden also of ancient lineage" during his boyhood. There is also a painting in the Rowe family's collection that is thought to be of the garden at 14 Priory Road, on the back of which is written, "I Remember I Remember where I used to swing". This suggests that Arthur looked back affectionately on his early years.

These cheerful recollections aside, the Lambeth of Arthur's boyhood was not a healthy place in which to grow up. Lambeth was an industrial as well as a residential area and the local potteries and glass works[2] had a negative impact on the environment. The streets that Arthur walked were dirty and dusty, and the air was often thick with smog. There was a gas works a few streets away from the family home, and the ever-present 'pea souper' took its toll on the health of Arthur's father and probably had a long-term impact on Arthur's health as well. In a letter to his son in 1884, Thomas George wrote about the subject:

> *This is a wretched foggy morning and it is having an effect upon me. I am suffering much with my breath. So I did last night for it was cold and they heaped up the fire while the heat arrived by the Gas almost did for me. The effect is very depressing and makes me almost despair of getting about again.*

Thomas George Rowe died the following year and Arthur in turn suffered from various lung complaints throughout his life.

Arthur was educated at Priory Grove School until the age of sixteen. He showed early promise in art as a boy and was awarded a certificate at the age of fifteen in freehand drawing, practical geometry, linear perspective and model drawing by the Department of Committee of the Council of Education. It appears that Arthur understood his strengths and weaknesses from a young age and applied himself to the subjects that held the most interest for him. He later compared his education to that of his son Ronald, writing,

> *I did not grasp properly what did not interest me very much.*
> *He is quick enough in the things I did well at I think —*
> *geography, drawing & calculation.*

With the likely heavy encouragement of his father, and with the help of family friend Frank Butterworth, Arthur began work as an apprentice lithographer after leaving school. Printing was a growing trade, and lithography was a good, steady profession for a young Victorian lad and one in which Thomas George probably felt that his son could utilise his natural artistic ability. Thomas George paid fifty-five pounds, a not inconsiderable sum at that time, for his son to begin a five-year term as an indentured apprentice lithographer in October 1878. At Montague Chatterton and Co in Grays Inn Road, Middlesex (now in north London) young Arthur learned the craft of drawing with grease on to a treated piece of stone to create the original artworks that were used in the printing of book illustrations.[3]

Many of the prints that were made using Arthur's originals are still in existence and he clearly excelled in his work, but lithography was not satisfying or challenging him. Even then he had a desire to paint. He wrote about his apprenticeship to Sophy in 1896:

> *...served five years (not in prison) but articled to a Crown Lithographer — at the end of my time I was a sort of jack of all its branches and master of none consequently I wasn't worth much and as I wanted a change I left — all this time I wanted to learn to paint but saw no chance — though I spent the one or two weeks holiday I had every summer trying to sketch.*

At some time during this period Arthur submitted two of his 'sketches' — the name he often used when referring to watercolour paintings — to the Royal Institute of Painters in Water Colours, which was about to open its doors to students at its new school in Piccadilly. Arthur's ambition to become an artist would not be quelled, and he was keeping abreast of developments in the world of fine art in the hope that he could get a foot in the door somehow.

But the problem of what he was to do until then would not go away, and Arthur could not free himself from the grip of lithography so easily. Two months after leaving his first job Arthur took up another lithography position, presumably after some pressure from his father whose money, after all, had paid for his son's initial training. Thomas George would not have wanted to see his investment come to nothing and probably persuaded Arthur to take another job in the same field in the hope that this time he would stick at it. He was to be disappointed: this

Two lithographs by Ernest Arthur Rowe

job only lasted for a month, as Arthur later explained: "there was no work to do and I got the sack and left Feb 2nd."

Just two days after Arthur was sacked, an event occurred that was to change his fortunes dramatically and would lead the aspiring artist down a new and more promising path. On Monday 4 February 1884 the Royal Institute of Painters in Water Colours opened its school. The paintings that Arthur had submitted to the institute had been deemed to be of a sufficiently high standard and on the basis of them, at the age of twenty-two, he was accepted as a probationer at the school. He wrote about it in a letter to Sophy in 1896:

> *I never supposed for a moment that I should ever be able to work there. I thought I would start work until I heard of something else — in two months I had passed my probation and was admitted as a student for two years.*

Arthur's initial self-doubt was unjustified. The tutors at the Royal Institute of Painters in Water Colours' school recognised that Arthur had talent, be it raw and unrefined, and accepted him with open arms. Although he had encouraged his son into lithography, Thomas George was supportive of this move, initially at least, as Arthur went on to state, "My father was alive then so of course I was living at home with few expenses."

But some event occurred during this time to distract Arthur from his path, as in September of the same year he left London for Middlesbrough to take a position in the field of lithography again. This must have been deeply disappointing for young Arthur after he had finally begun to work towards his goal of becoming a professional artist. Additionally, he was used to being surrounded by a tightly knit circle of friends and family. To find himself in this rapidly expanding industrial northern town without his support network, and forced to go back to a job he loathed, must have been painful. It was not the right move for Arthur, and he stayed in Middlesbrough for just three months before returning to London and the Royal Institute school.

During his two years at the school Arthur experimented with his subject matter painting, for example, scenes from the village of Clovelly in Devon. But as early as 1884 he travelled to a house, the garden of which would become prominent in Arthur's later work, namely Penshurst Place in Kent. Sir Henry Sidney had constructed this garden, with its distinctive walls and

Formal Garden, Penshurst, Kent 1885

terraces, during the Elizabethan era. After a period of neglect, the house was inherited by the 2nd Lord De L'Isle of Dudley in 1851 who set about restoring the garden to its former glory. One of the main features that he introduced was the mile-long yew hedge that divided up the garden into a series of rooms, each with its individual style.[4] In one early painting of Penshurst by Arthur, entitled *The Orange Court,* the garden is neglected entirely, as the artist focused on the house itself (in contrast to Arthur's later work). There is no sign in this painting of the vibrant colours that would fill Arthur's 'sketches' in later years. Also, in *The Orange Court* Arthur followed the fashion of including figures in eighteenth-century costume. In the following year, the artist painted Penshurst Place again in a work that he called *Formal Garden.* In this painting, the house is relegated to the background while the garden is given prominence. Despite this, there is still not the slightest hint of colour other than greens and browns in the painting, with the artist concentrating instead on the geometric shapes of the hedges and pathways of this meticulously designed garden.

It is not clear whether or not Arthur had to pay to attend the Royal Institute school. If he did, it is possible that he had some financial assistance from his father, or he may have sold the odd painting here and there to see him through. In any case, the problem of funding became more acute in March 1885 with the death of Arthur's father. Thomas George left each of his five children two hundred pounds in his will, but despite this financial cushion Arthur realised at this point in his life that he would have to, "think about making money somehow". The relatively carefree existence that he had enjoyed during his boyhood and early adulthood was over. Things were about to get serious for Ernest Arthur Rowe.

The young artist decided that the best thing that he could do at the time was to put his money into bricks and mortar. With the two hundred pounds that was left to him, combined with sixty pounds borrowed from his mother, Arthur purchased 9 Placquett Road, East Dulwich (now 150 Copleston Road, Camberwell). This was the first of several houses that Arthur would buy over the years, and they proved to be wise investments as the rents from some of his properties would later come in very useful when work was thin on the ground.

Financial insecurity aside, Arthur was about to achieve the first major success of his career, although it must have pained him that he was not able to share his success with his father. In May 1885 he was awarded the President's medal for landscape, issued by the Royal Institute of Painters in Water Colours. This beautifully embossed silver medal was awarded to the artist for an unknown painting of an old garden. Arthur modestly said of the prize in a letter in 1896 to his future wife that he "got it much to my own surprise and everybody else's", although to win this award from such a prestigious institution was clearly a measure of Arthur's obvious talent, even as a fledgling painter. This medal, which is still in the Rowe family, is an exceptional object in itself being the only one of its kind ever awarded by the Royal Institute. Arthur stayed on as a student for another year but in May 1886 the Royal Institute school closed, although the institute continued to exhibit paintings at its Piccadilly gallery and still exists to this day.

In the summer of 1885, perhaps to divert his mind from his grief at the death of his father, perhaps simply motivated by money or the lack of it, Arthur began to work feverishly. He travelled around the south of England from Kent to Devon for seven weeks with a paintbrush in his hand almost continually. He explained this period to Sophy in 1896 by saying that he spent

The Royal Institute of Painters in Water Colours' President's medal for landscape, 1885

The Girl's Head (above right) and another of Arthur's early portraits (above)

these weeks "working from 6 in the morning till 9 at night — until I couldn't see". This dedication to his art paid off, as Arthur sold a number of paintings and earned the grand sum of ninety pounds that year.

With Arthur's studies cut short by the closure of the Royal Institute school, he looked for an alternative academy of learning. Before long he was accepted as a student at the Lambeth School of Art and he studied there almost every evening and many Saturday mornings for the following ten years. At the Lambeth school he practised portraiture among other things; the school regularly hired models for the students to sketch. Some of Arthur's early black-and-white portraits still exist and they show that he was just as adept at painting people as he was at painting gardens. He complained later in a letter to Sophy that portrait painters earned more money than garden painters. Perhaps he had a minor regret that he had not chosen this career path, for he would surely have had just as much success in it as he had in the painting of gardens.

Encouraged by his initial commercial success in the summer of 1885, Arthur continued to paint at a ferocious pace with the expectancy that he would sell every painting that he produced. He would even make several copies of some of the original works, each one slightly smaller than the one before, in anticipation of finding a market for them. Years later, though, he confessed to Sophy that he had used up all his friends, and although he had thought that he was going to make his fortune, reality had quickly bitten: "after that they didn't want any more, so I managed to rub along and made about £100 a year."

Times became very hard for Arthur, and although he continued to paint almost non-stop, the work still did not have any real focus and Arthur had not yet succeeded in making a name for himself.

The artist at this time used much more muted hues than he would employ in his later works, notably in *Evening Light* — a delightful oil painting of Tinker's Cottage in Boscastle, which effectively portrays a warm Cornish summer's evening and which Arthur exhibited at the Royal Academy. In another example of an early work entitled *The Old Dovecot,* Arthur appears to have experimented with symbolism. The scene depicts a child digging a grave for a dead bird, possibly a reference to events outside the world of the painting.

With the commercial success that he had hoped for

Right: Evening Light, 1889

Left: The Old Dovecot, Maresfield, East Sussex, 1888

eluding him, Arthur found himself slipping into debt in the years 1887–1891. It was only with the financial support of both his mother and his sister, Florence, that he was able to carry on working and studying during these years. Money was so tight that he was often unable to afford the bus fares and would walk for miles just to save a penny.

Arthur had some recognition from the art establishment during this period, winning silver medals from the Dover School of Art in 1889 and 1890 for his watercolour work. Annually works were submitted to the South Kensington School of Art by various art schools around the country. These works of art would then be judged by government examiners, who awarded twelve gold medals, thirty silver medals and sixty bronze medals each year. So Arthur's work must have beaten hundreds of other paintings to win his two silver medals, yet art buyers were still not taking the bait. In his letters to Sophy, Arthur described 1890 as his most "disastrous year" when he made just over thirty pounds and he was forced to borrow ninety pounds from his sister, Florence. Things were looking bleak for this young artist. With no real direction to his work and a limited market for the kinds of paintings that he was producing, Arthur seemed to be digging deeper and deeper into a pit of financial ruin. Then in 1891 he decided to paint gardens full-time and his fortunes finally changed.

Chapter two

VICTORIAN GARDENS

the glory of the garden glorifieth every one
Rudyard Kipling

The Victorians were passionate about their gardens. Aristocratic landowners hired huge teams of gardeners to design and plant the great formal gardens reproduced in such fine detail by artists like Arthur, George Samuel Elgood and Beatrice Parsons. Using different styles and often non-native plants, innovative garden designers would lay out their gardens on a grand scale. Sometimes they would divide large gardens into separate 'rooms', each with its own unique style, like the garden at Penshurst Place.[5] Whatever their tastes, wealthy garden owners were able to let their imaginations run wild and created extravagant landscape gardens for their year-round enjoyment.

But gardening was no longer solely a hobby of the upper classes. The influence of William Morris and others in the Arts and Crafts movement was broad. The Victorians had witnessed the brutal industrialisation of their country over a few short years. Blake's "green and pleasant land" had changed immeasurably, and the likes of John Ruskin and Morris developed their theories in part as a reaction to these changes. As a counterbalance to the factories and mills that were spreading across Britain, Morris and others encouraged people to cultivate plants and flowers. Moreover, many influential gardeners in the late Victorian era such as William Robinson favoured a return to using native plants and flowers.[6] Around the country, in the late nineteenth century and early twentieth century, garden cities such as Port Sunlight in Merseyside, Bournville in Birmingham, and London's Hampstead Garden Suburb were developed. In these new villages, designed to accommodate the ordinary worker, each cottage came with its own garden where working class men and women were encouraged to create their own miniature Eden.

The Royal Horticultural Society had been founded in 1804. In 1888 it held its first Temple Show in Central London (a forerunner of today's Chelsea Flower Show). This proved to be a success despite torrential rain. Floral displays by amateurs and commercial firms alike were put up in two large marquees. The show became a yearly fixture and by 1897 the two marquees had become five, with additional displays out in the open air.[7]

The surge of interest in gardening at this time led to an increase in reading material published for the amateur gardener. Numerous journals were produced to satisfy the public's interest in the subject such as *The Gardener's Chronicle* and *The Garden*. To satisfy the demand for information, a large number of gardening books were also published during this period, many by the 'celebrity' gardeners of the day such as William Robinson and Gertrude Jekyll.

So Arthur's decision to dedicate himself to the painting of gardens was probably influenced by the excitement about gardening that he witnessed among his friends, family and the people around him. After experiencing the soot, smog and grime that was part and parcel of this newly industrialised nation, the idea of retreating into a peaceful, picturesque garden in the countryside, far away from the factories and the smoke, must have been more appealing than ever. Gardens were now most definitely in vogue and Arthur would have been aware of this when he decided to devote his time to the painting of them.

Arthur's canny appreciation of the public's mood was integral to his success as a garden painter, but the importance of

Christine Hamlyn to Arthur's career cannot be overstated. Arthur first visited Clovelly in Devon in 1885 and it seems likely that this was when they first met. Mrs Hamlyn was a very wealthy landowner. As well as being lady of the manor house, Clovelly Court, she owned the entire village including every house, shop, inn and even the fishing port, as well as all the surrounding land. She took an interest in everything that went on in her village, paid for many bright local children's schooling, and kept a record of all the details in large scrapbooks that she called *The Clovelly Chronicles.* In these volumes, Mrs Hamlyn meticulously added newspaper cuttings and other documents about anything that was of local interest. Over the years she included a number of articles about Arthur and his work, and there are still at least three of his paintings hanging in the house.

On Arthur's first visit to Clovelly he had spent his time painting general views of the village including the Red Lion, the harbour and the post office. When she became aware that a talented artist was in the village, Mrs Hamlyn decided that it would be a good idea to ask him to record the big house with his brush, so she invited Arthur to paint Clovelly Court.

The majestic house sits at the top of a steep hill, which runs right down to the picturesque port, and oversees the village, port and sea beyond. Arthur's first invitation there marked the beginning of an influential friendship that was to last until his death, and Arthur returned to Clovelly many times over the years. Mrs Hamlyn and her husband Frederick Hamlyn had a wide social circle that included aristocratic families up and down the country. They introduced Arthur to a number of their friends and actively helped to gain permission for Arthur to paint their gardens. This is illustrated by a letter that Lord Frederick wrote to Arthur in 1895:

> *At last I have received a reply from Mr. Watson's sister Lady Seymour granting access for you to sketch etc. etc. Rockingham Castle. Lady Seymour's writing is so bad that you will have some difficulty in reading her letter which keep. I do not want it back. In the letter you will gather that all you have to do is introduce yourself to the Housekeeper, Mrs. Dean, at Rockingham and she will give you information and open the house for you.*

Arthur later acknowledged the importance of these influential

Clovelly Post Office, 1885

people to his career, explaining in a letter to his wife just after they had met that he had "got in with a good set of people". After 1891, with the help of the Hamlyns, he began to spend his time flitting from one beautiful English garden to another like an industrious bee, in order to paint the flowers of the gentry. Sometimes a wealthy garden owner would commission Arthur to paint his or her garden. If he was not specifically commissioned to paint on an estate, he would travel to the eminent houses on his "own book" and often still sell a painting or two to the owner who would be delighted to hang the flattering reproduction on a wall in the house as a reminder of his or her garden in its summertime splendour.

These garden paintings have a lighter tone than Arthur's previous work. Gone are the thick oils that Arthur had used in paintings like *A Winter's Tale,* which depicts a snow-covered Rye in Sussex. Arthur's new style is colourful and bright. The viewer is no longer asked to observe the scene from a distance. In these paintings, the viewer is invited to step right into the scene. With his generous use of light and shade combined with a meticulous attention to detail, the artist welcomes the viewer into each of the gardens that he depicts. One example of this is a painting called *Under the Apple Trees.* This is a representation of the garden of a house called Old Place in Lindfield, Sussex, and was painted in 1901. The scene shows a perfect lawn leading to the old timbered house. The lawn acts as an emerald path directing the viewer towards the warm and inviting rust coloured building. At either side of the lawn are flowerbeds spilling over with a multitude of pink, red and orange blooms. On the outside of each of these beds are rows of formal hedges enclosing the little garden, giving it a feeling of security and secrecy. A small child is tending to the flowers, adding a charming feeling of innocence to the scene, while a little dog looks on from the distance. This whole painting has a golden glow to it, which is typical of Arthur's mature work. The artist always began a painting with a yellow wash, which helped to achieve this warmth of tone. Finally, as the title of the painting suggests, there are apple trees at the outer edges of the painting, one of which is out of view, although the dappled shade that falls over the foreground makes the viewer believe that there is more beauty to explore within this garden, outside the boundaries of the painting.

Arthur took great advantage of one of the crowning achievements of the Victorian era, the British railway system,

A Winter's Tale, Rye

Under the Apple Trees, Old Place, Lindfield, Sussex, 1901

which had been developed over the previous few decades. From his home in Placquett Road, Arthur was able to travel by train all over the country, putting his trusty bicycle in the guard's van. Strapped to his bicycle would be everything he needed for his work — easel, paints, brushes and umbrella — and he would take the train to the nearest stop. From there he would cycle the last few miles to his destination. From 1891 onwards he worked almost continually, painting the grand gardens of Penshurst Place, Compton Wynyates in Warwickshire, Helmingham Hall in Suffolk, Montacute in Somerset and more.

Like the garden at Penshurst Place, the garden at Compton Wynyates had suffered from neglect for many years until the late Victorian period when the magnificent topiary and lawns were added and both the house and gardens were restored to something of their former grandeur.[8] There was much of interest in this garden for Arthur, who returned to paint it again and again. The garden at Montacute, named after the nearby conical hill, or 'Mons Acutis', incorporated the yew hedging that Arthur was so fond of, and Helmingham Hall was a magnificent moated house with acres of gardens for the artist to explore and locate the perfect view.[9]

In 1907 the interviewer from *The Girl's Realm* magazine asked Arthur to analyse and interpret the charm of an old formal garden:

> *Perhaps the best answer is that it reveals a well-ordered classic restraint. But within this restraint there is still a place for the lavish blossoming of nature unarranged, as well as for the flowering of the ordered blooms.*

The coexistence of order and "nature unarranged" is clear within all of Arthur's garden paintings. Often the scene will incorporate formal clipped yew hedges, finely manicured lawns or grand balustrades. But the paintings will also include borders of brightly coloured blooms exuberantly spilling over the edges of the borders, breaking up the formal lines. Or Arthur would achieve a sense of informality with the inclusion of figures, particularly animals and children. The inclusion of these figures, lacking in the trait of self-awareness that most adults have, adds a natural touch to the paintings, breaking up the almost-severe formality of some of the gardens and increasing the sense of realism.

The incidental characters that appear in Arthur's paintings

usually simply walked into view as the artist worked. There was no prearrangement with the models; they merely happened to be in the garden at the moment when Arthur was committing the scene to paper. At Levens Hall in Cumbria, famed for its elaborate topiary some of which is among the oldest in the world[10], Arthur painted the head gardener's daughter who fortuitously ran across the grass while he was at his easel. With her untamed red ringlets, the child would have made an interesting subject for the artist. When the child's mother realised that her daughter was going to be in a painting, she rushed over to tidy the girl up, telling her to smooth out her dress and pull up her socks. Arthur, however, told her not to change a thing about her appearance; he wanted to paint her just as he saw her, with all her childish charm. This painting — a great example of Arthur's love of formality combined with "nature unarranged" — was exhibited in the Royal Academy.

Now thirty, when he was not working Arthur continued with his studies spending any free moment at the Lambeth School of Art, and he continued to study and improve his skills throughout his life. When Arthur was not studying or painting, he was usually immersed in the world of art, visiting exhibitions of paintings or spending time with his fellow students. In his one surviving diary, from 1892, Arthur detailed his daily life. Here Arthur mentioned working at the Natural History Museum, where he may have been studying the plants. He also talked about painting Waterloo Station and visiting Hampton Court Palace, "to look for artefacts". Hampton Court and its gardens later became a favourite place of work for Arthur; he painted the palace and its grounds on numerous occasions in the latter part of his career.

In the 1892 diary, Arthur talked about visiting several galleries including the National Gallery, the Royal Academy, and the New Gallery where he viewed an exhibition of the pre-Raphaelite painter Edward Burne-Jones. But an indication was also given of his feeling towards the new modern styles of painting that were coming into fashion in parallel to the traditional realism of Arthur and others. The New English Art Club, founded in 1886, favoured a more impressionistic, less traditional, style of art.[11] Arthur summed up his feeling in one word when he wrote about it on 28 December: "Went to New English Art Club in morning (disgusted) and from there to RWS."

During the latter nineteenth century a large number of exhibition societies and sketching clubs came into being. These provided facilities for artists including studios and exhibition space, and offered them alternative venues to the Royal Academy to showcase their work.[12] Arthur was a member of at least two sketching clubs; he mentioned both the Suffolk Street Sketch Club and the London Sketch Club in his 1892 diary. Like many other up-and-coming artists, Arthur was able to put the facilities offered by these clubs to good use, as well as finding a new and larger audience for his work.

Arthur's friends at this time were largely other artists whom he had met at the Lambeth School of Art. These included the painters Alfred Moore, George Edward Robertson and Henry Terry, but the most successful of Arthur's circle was the illustrator Arthur Rackham, who also studied alongside Arthur at the Lambeth School of Art. In his 1892 diary Arthur talked about visiting his friend at his studio and meeting him in Penshurst where they were both working, and staying at the same guesthouse. While Arthur continued to paint realistic garden watercolours, his friend found success in the field of book illustration, painting intricate imaginative scenes for both children's and adults' books.

Although each entry is brief, Arthur's 1892 diary tells us much about the artist and his dedication to his work. One thing it clearly shows is how much Arthur was at the mercy of the elements and how aware he was of the importance of fine weather. Each entry begins with a brief description of Arthur's day and each ends, without fail, with a weather report. Often rain would frustrate Arthur's plans. For example, Arthur wrote on 19 August:

> *Worked in garden under an umbrella in morning and for an hour in afternoon then gave it up as a bad job. Rained all day.*

On 25 August, he commented that it was a "Grey day in the morning". On 21 May, frustration led to ruin when painting at Penshurst and a "24x20 drawing blown into fishpond". Although Arthur's paintings appear serene and calm, life for a Victorian garden painter was never easy.

The Pond in the Formal Garden, Penshurst, 1921

Chapter three

LOVE AND MARRIAGE

She was a phantom of delight
When first she gleam'd upon my sight
William Wordsworth

Arthur continued to work hard and build up a good customer base, and he continued to take the train all over the country from Montacute in Somerset to Melbourne Hall in Derbyshire. There was no let-up in the pace of work and he produced paintings by the dozen. The motto of the Lambeth Art School — 'If I rest I rust' — was taken literally.

As he sold more paintings, Arthur was able to pay back the money he had borrowed from his mother and sister, Flo, during the difficult years of 1887–1891. In 1895 Arthur sold a painting for the princely sum of sixty-eight pounds and was able to pay off his debts completely. Finally in the black at the age of thirty-three, Arthur saw an opportunity to build on his success, to earn money as an artist and to forge ahead with his chosen career. He understood the market for garden paintings, he had made numerous useful connections thanks to Mrs Hamlyn, and his skills as a watercolourist were at their peak. Nothing was going to get in his way on his journey to becoming a successful artist. The world was his, or so it seemed.

Of course things in life are rarely that simple and the problem of Arthur's poor health was not going to go away. Arthur's lungs were ravaged by what the Victorians termed 'consumption', now known as tuberculosis (TB), and he struggled with the cold, damp English winters. Arthur was continually underweight and coughing, and this dreadful disease weakened his body if not his spirit. Travelling and working at the pace that he did took its toll on his health as well, not to mention the stress he would have endured knowing that he must work to pay his bills and keep his head above water. There was a limit to the amount that his mother and sister could do to support him — in fact he was by now supporting them — and there was no wealthy family to bail Arthur out if he got into long term financial difficulties.

In 1895 Arthur's doctor suggested that he make a trip to the Fluela Sanatorium at Davos in Switzerland. The clean Swiss mountain air was considered to be highly beneficial for the lungs of TB patients. Thousands made the trip to the sanatorium in the late nineteenth century in the hope that they could be cured of this debilitating disease. One patient was the writer Robert Louis Stevenson who completed *Treasure Island* during his time there.[13] As Arthur had recently sold a painting for such a large sum he was able to pay for the trip, and he decided that it might be just what he needed.

Arthur stayed in Davos for five months, from October 1895 to March 1896, and it was at the sanatorium that he first met a young nurse called Sophy Annie Slater. Before her arrival the new nurse was the talk of the sanatorium and the guests were excited by the idea of meeting the new employee. Arthur and his friends wondered aloud whether she would be pretty or not, whether she would be kind or cruel, and Arthur admitted later that he was hopeful that she would turn out to be his soulmate: "I didn't love you from the first it came very gradual, after you came I had a sort of longing that you would turn out to be someone whom I could love…then we all liked your face when you arrived and thought that you were a very sweet little thing."

Sophy was born in New South Wales, Australia. Hers was

Above: Sophy Slater and Ernest Arthur Rowe at the Fluela Pass, Davos, 1895
Right: Sophy Slater, 1896

a family of missionaries — her father was a Baptist minister and staunchly religious, and Sophy was expected to follow the family tradition and spread Christianity to the far corners of the world. Sophy's mother had died at sea on the way to England from Australia, when her only child was still a babe in arms, and Sophy's father had married again providing Sophy with several stepsisters.

His first meeting with the young nurse made a lasting impression on Arthur. "I often think of my first glance of you as you came into the dining room," he later wrote. They seem to have been attracted to each other from the start and, although neither declared their love until later, there was a certain amount of intimacy between the pair even in the early months of their friendship.

As they played out their respective roles of patient and carer, deep feelings began to develop within them both. Several times in later letters Arthur referred to an idyllic day when they rode on a toboggan together through the snowy landscape around the Swiss sanatorium. "I believe one of the happiest times I spent with you at Davos," wrote Arthur, "was when I had you that night on the toboggan and put my arms round your waist — the nearest approach to an embrace I was then permitted."

Perhaps prudish Victorian convention got the better of Arthur or perhaps he was overtaken by shyness, as Arthur's feelings for the young nurse were consuming him but he was not able to declare his love for Sophy during their time together at Davos. He later wrote: "If I had only been sure that things would have come out all right I should have kissed you then and there and have made you confess that you loved me for I know you did then even if you did not know it." Arthur left Davos in March without expressing his true feelings, but he and Sophy continued to correspond with one another.

In April 1896 Arthur visited Italy for the first time and wrote to Sophy from Rome. Sophy told Arthur that she planned to travel to Paris from Davos in order to undertake missionary work, helping the city's poor. Arthur said that she should not go, ostensibly because the work would be too much for her but perhaps really motivated by the sense that the pull of religion might pull her away from him. He made no bones about the way he felt about the idea in a letter, saying:

I am sorry to hear of your idea about mission work in Paris.

> *I don't think that Paris will suit you at all, you will only knock yourself up again — I hope for your sake when you next write to hear that it is off — so please write soon & let me know all about it & what the work is.*

Following this letter, Arthur must have received a stern response from Nurse Slater, as in a subsequent letter he apologised to his future wife, writing,

> *Again I must ask you to forgive me, for I'm afraid I have given you pain where I had no intention of doing so. I certainly am interested in your Mission work and shall always be in anything that you do. The reason why I said that 'I did not like the idea of your doing mission work in Paris' was, that I don't believe that you are strong enough to bear such a strain as I know working in the east end of Paris must be and though you are A.1. at looking after other people's comfort you are far too unselfish to look after yourself. I kept my eyes open when I was in Davos!*

Despite Arthur's objections Sophy did not change her plans. She travelled from Davos to Paris where she started work at a temperance boarding house, a "rambling old place" offering succour to the poor and helpless who found themselves in the French capital. Sophy did not speak French fluently but was determined to learn the language so that she could carry out her work more effectively.

National borders separated the young friends, but Arthur was very keen to see Sophy again. She had made such an impression on him in Davos that he found it impossible to remove her from his thoughts day and night. With his pen he tentatively suggested that he might visit her on his return journey to England from Italy. In this letter he talked about all the sightseeing that he would like to do in Paris, but his real reason for the detour was clear:

> *I expect I shall start about May 18th and go through Paris — I should like to have a day in Paris and rush through the Salon, the Louvres and see the gardens of Versailles. I wonder if it is possible — I suppose you could not spare a couple of hours to take me to the latter place? This is only a suggestion and I can quite understand that it would not*

do, as you have been where you are such a short time. Please say just what you think about it. I should be sorry to stop at Paris and not see you but at the same time I should not like to make things awkward — I suppose I could not put up at your Temperance Boarding House? I should feel under your protection then.

The response was not at all what Arthur had hoped for or anticipated. Without explanation, Sophy rejected Arthur's suggestions entirely and said no to him visiting her at all, instead recommending a few hotels in Paris where he might find lodging. Not only did she tell him that she did not want to see him but she added that he must not write to her again. Arthur was stunned, as the fledgling romance faltered. He did not believe that he had misread the mood and invented the spark between them, and he wrote to Sophy expressing his devastation at her rejection:

On receiving your letter this morning I must say that at first I was quite simply stunned, not at your not being able to meet me, I quite see as you see, that it would be awkward for you, and I don't blame you in the very least. If anything I admire you all the more for being so candid and saying just what you thought. What really staggered me was 'that it would be best for all correspondence to cease'.

Clearly feeling that he now had nothing to lose, Arthur became more candid about his emotions towards Sophy and continued,

I can see no possible reason why it should, unless you have ceased to care for me and I don't believe you have. This is presumptuous perhaps as I am a nobody and have no prospects, but I flatter myself that we understood one another.

Arthur felt, with good reason, that Sophy had trouble reconciling her growing feelings for the young artist with her love of God. Love for a man and love for God, in her eyes, seemed to be mutually exclusive. It was Arthur who put this idea into words, saying, "I can't help thinking that you have an idea that you must entirely sacrifice yourself to your cause and God forbid that I should be the means of leading you, directly or indirectly, from doing what is right." He went on to say that if it was truly her wish that he ceased writing to her he would, of course, respect that; he would do anything for her happiness. But he added, "at present all I can say is, God help me, for I feel rather 'hard hit'."

Arthur's bold tactic paid off. Just two days later Sophy answered his letter, and her true feelings finally poured out on to the page. In this letter she made a declaration of love:

> *About my love for you — I hardly dare speak or I do not know when or where I should end and besides it has been so interwoven with Paris that I feel as if the two would always be inseparable to my mind — and that neither will bear being talked of. But I will say just this — I do love you with all my heart, first and dearest and best of all. You have the first place in my heart next to my Master Christ. I felt as if I could not keep you in doubt about this or anything else, and I am very glad you believed in spite of my last letter 'that I cared for you still'. You must never doubt that, whatever happens or does not happen and I never will doubt it of you.*

Sophy went on to explain her reason for the earlier rejection. It stemmed, as Arthur had suspected, from her devout religious conviction. Coming from a family of missionaries, Sophy had dedicated her life so far to helping the poor, doing good works and spreading the word of God. This was, she believed, her destiny, and this exciting young artist had come into her life and disrupted all the plans that she had made. She explained that she had always had a strong desire to "go to the heathen" and going to Davos was designed to strengthen her in preparation for that future work. When she had found herself falling for Arthur she became confused, as her love of her work and feelings for Arthur clashed, and she "felt that one must be given up and I was fearfully perplexed but longed to do God's will hard as it was".

Feeling that her actions needed further explanation, Sophy went on to say that her father had advised her to apply to two Scottish missionary societies in the hope that she would join him in India, where he was working as a missionary, later that year. To her relief, Sophy's qualifications had not been sufficient and both societies had turned her down. Sophy saw this as the work of God. It was then that the idea of going to Paris had come up and Sophy had "rejoiced as it would not be so far from you, and thanked God for the idea". God, in Sophy's eyes, had intervened and she had "settled down quickly…and was so happy to think that God had not wanted me to give you up after all but had made a 'way of escape' in the sore heart trial which made it bearable in that he had given me work nearer home".

Then, to Sophy's bewilderment, God had appeared to change his mind. A friend from Birmingham wrote to her to say that a friend, a missionary, was shortly due to travel to China and was looking for a governess for her children. She had specifically asked for Sophy, whom she had met and whom she felt fitted the bill perfectly. This created another troubling dilemma for Sophy who was torn between her love for Arthur and the idea that she might go to China and benefit mankind. "I was simply overcome," she wrote, "with amazement and perplexity and knew not what to do."

Earnestly, Sophy had prayed to God for a sign or some guidance to help her make a decision about what to do. The sign had come in the form of a letter from Arthur, although he had not yet declared his feelings to her. With this assurance from God, Sophy had turned down the Chinese position to the confusion and surprise of her friends and family. Sophy, after all, had always been such a devout girl who wanted so dearly to help people. What could have happened? After her family and friends' bewildered reaction Sophy had then begun to doubt her judgement and wondered if Arthur really loved her after all. It was then that she had written to tell him to cease all correspondence, "as I felt it might hinder me in deciding as I would be tempted to listen to my own heart instead of to the heavenly voice for I was beginning to think (as you suggest) that perhaps after all God meant me to sacrifice myself and you and everything that meant happiness to 'the cause' — so I wrote to you — and oh the pain of that letter".

Then Arthur's letter had come, where his feelings became plain, and Sophy made a decision about her future. She could not travel to China and leave behind the man that she had grown to love so dearly. Arthur had won her heart, although Sophy still felt the seeds of doubt stirring in her soul. "It seemed as if it were to be a test of my love to Christ," she wrote, "and sometimes I wonder still if I am doing right to listen to the voice of my own heart."

Sophy's religious convictions were always clearly expressed and her deep love of God continued for the rest of her life. Arthur, in contrast, was not a particularly religious man. Like any other Victorian, he went to church every Sunday, although this seems to have been more from social necessity than any deep spiritual conviction. In a letter to Sophy in 1896 he spoke frankly about his religious beliefs:

> *I have never talked on religious matters & I can't quite fancy myself, Sophy mine. I've been indifferent on that subject as are a good many others. I'm sorry to say, and as I said before, it is difficult to change one's spots and mine are very black and I can't get them out.*

In the same letter, Arthur went on to talk about a future meeting with Sophy's aunts and his hopes that they would not quiz him on religious matters:

> *As to the epistles to the Ephesians I must tell the honest truth and admit that I don't enjoy them. I believe the only parts of the New Testament that I really seem to grasp are the four Gospels and the Revelations. I expect it will give you pain to hear it but I had better tell you than let you have a false impression of me. I sincerely hope that your Aunts will not open at all on religious subjects or they will see a very weak side of me.*

Neither Arthur nor Sophy told their families about each other for some time after they had declared their love. Arthur was worried about his mother's natural tendency to disapprove of everything initially until she came round to the idea. "My mother will make objections," he penned, "(I don't mean as regards to you) and would no matter who I chose, for it is in her nature to." His mother's deafness was also referred to by Arthur as a reason to put off telling his mother:

> *I have not told my mother yet, the great secret, the opportunity hasn't offered itself. I want her at home alone — it is awfully awkward as I have to shout out everything and the walls are so thin that they can hear next door what is said. Imagine how difficult it is to talk about this sort of thing at the top of your voice.*

Sophy wanted to tell her father, the Reverend Thomas Ebenezer Slater, about Arthur, but she was concerned that this highly religious man would not be happy about the relationship. Coming from a respectable ecclesiastical family of a high social standing, there was the problem of Arthur's chosen career to consider. An artist in the early stages of his career was not a terribly solid prospect and would not perhaps be a minister's first choice as a son-in-law. Arthur himself acknowledged this when writing to Sophy early in their relationship and asked her to wait for two or three years before they married to enable him to establish himself financially: "you can see that I am also very poor, can you hope on and love on for two or three years until prospects brighten a bit and pray that they may for your sake as well as my own."

On top of the lack of money there was thc question of Arthur's health. Any father would want his daughter to choose a husband who would be able to provide for her in the long term. Arthur, with his weak TB-ridden lungs, did not appear to be a man capable of looking after a wife and children for a great many years hence. Arthur could see the serious risk that Sophy was taking with her future and wrote that she had offered to wreck her own life for him, although he continued to hold out hope that his health would improve. "I do hope to get better and I pray God that I may, for your sake and my own," he continued. Both Arthur and Sophy were well aware that their future comfort was hanging by a thread. Late nineteenth century Britain was not an easy place to live in without a decent income. In one letter Arthur even half-joked about how the couple might end up in the poor house. The social convention of the time was that the man of the house would look after his family financially. If the worst occurred and Arthur's health did not improve, he spoke frankly about the likely outcome: "If I get no better it would mean in a year or two that I should cease to do any work and should soon be penniless, then the misery that would come on your innocent little head makes me shudder to think of it."

With all these concerns in mind Arthur and Sophy did not get engaged immediately, Arthur preferring to wait until he felt healthier and stronger and more certain of being able to look after his "darling little Sophy".

Arthur and Sophy's fears about her father's reaction were justified. When Sophy finally told the Reverend Slater, who was still living in India at the time, about the man she loved he did not immediately warm to the idea of his daughter's new relationship. To Sophy, he wrote that she should not "love on with no hope of marriage", clearly not anticipating any great improvement in Arthur's prospects or health.

Arthur, speaking to Sophy in a language that she could understand, responded by saying that they must, *go on loving one another & wait for God to decide. It is quite certain that he will decide in the next two or three years and we hope for the best my darling, so cheer up.*

Despite Sophy's father's disapproval, the pair continued to correspond. Sophy stayed on in Paris while Arthur lived in London and travelled far and wide to work, and the young sweethearts met up whenever they could.

The artist was never off duty, and in these early letters Arthur would make little comments about Sophy's appearance and dress. In one letter he suggested that she wore a large black hat rather than the little white hat that she owned and that he did not like, saying that a "black hat would suit you splendidly, if it has a nice broad brim". He went on to ask her forgiveness for commenting on her dress and said that he did not intend to be rude, but that he had "got in the habit of looking critically on things because I've been asked my opinion so often". In a subsequent letter, Arthur explained at length why he thought that Sophy would look better in a dress with a high waist rather than a low waist. His reasoning was based on the traditional belief among artists that "a third plays a more important part than a half". Where the low-waisted dress cut the figure in two, the high waist drew the eye to a point a third of the way down the body, and this was naturally more aesthetically pleasing. Arthur even accompanied his ideas with a little sketch of the two dresses to illustrate his point and ended by joking, "I hope that you won't think that this two pages on 'waists' is altogether 'wasted'." *(See next page.)*

Although Arthur felt that he was able to give an opinion on Sophy's clothes, their relationship in general was a modern one where both partners were equal. Fairly unusually for the times, Arthur did not expect to be the lord and master of his family and hoped that Sophy would share the responsibility for decision making within their little family unit. Looking to the future, Arthur wrote about the kind of marriage that Sophy could expect, saying:

My own, my remark about your obeying me was, of course, a joke — it would not do for you to obey me in all things, apart from conscience, as far as giving commands go I don't think that you would ever find me a severe master, though I don't like the word master at all. I should want you to be the ruler

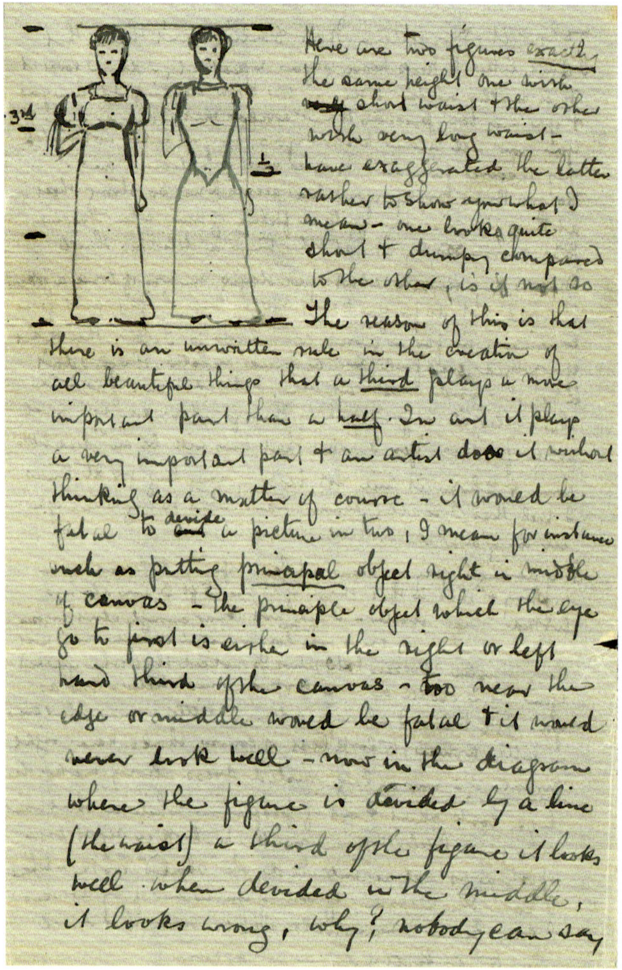

3rd — ½ —

Here are two figures exactly the same height one with short waist & the other with very long waist — have exaggerated the latter rather to show you what I mean — one looks quite short & dumpy compared to the other, is it not so The reason of this is that there is an unwritten rule in the creation of all beautiful things that a third plays a more important part than a half. In art it plays a very important part & an artist does it without thinking as a matter of course — it would be fatal to divide a picture in two, I mean for instance such as putting principal object right in middle of canvas — the principle object which the eye go to first is either in the right or left hand third of the canvas — too near the edge or middle would be fatal & it would never look well — now in the diagram where the figure is divided by a line (the waist) a third of the figure it looks well when divided in the middle, it looks wrong, why? nobody can say

in a good many things it would be much better for me.

Sophy's father's worries about Arthur must have eventually been quelled, as the pair continued to correspond and sealed their relationship by becoming engaged in 1897, just a year after their first meeting. By then Sophy was back in England working as a governess.

In 1898 Arthur moved to 42 Edward Street in Southborough near Tunbridge Wells with his mother and sister, Flo. Arthur had long had a desire to move out of London to somewhere where the air was cleaner, in the hope that it would benefit his ailing lungs. With his family connections in the area (Arthur had numerous aunts, uncles and cousins living nearby) Tunbridge Wells was an obvious choice, although he complained to Sophy about the extended family, writing, "this afternoon am expecting a lot of cousins who I'm not very anxious to see — nothing in common — another hindrance." Arthur felt the new house was small and modest, saying,

Things in the new house fit pretty well but there does not seem much room anywhere. It is about as interesting a looking

house outside as you would see in a day's march — house did I call it? Cottage!

Arthur was proved right about the health benefits of his new situation, as his breathing became greatly improved away from the smog of the city. Shortly after the move he wrote to Sophy about Southborough Common, which he found beautiful: "Am getting on — yesterday being fine I went out up on the common for an hour or so & feel very well bar cough, which is not troublesome during the day but mostly at night." He commented that a respected doctor sent his patients to the area, as it was "high and all sandy". Altogether Arthur was very positive about the move from London, and the only problem with his new situation was that there were "too many relations".

Unfortunately life behind the scenes for some of Arthur's relations had become very hard by this time. Arthur's elder brother, George, was on the other side of the world in Tasmania. George had had a varied career and did not seem to be able to settle in any profession. The list of the various businesses that he had been involved in so far was extensive and included a chemist's, a firm of solicitors and a wood engraving company. Arthur's brother had also tried his hand at being a seedsman and a farmer. Annie, Arthur's eldest sister, had married a widower with two girls who were, according to Arthur, "the bane of her existence". Florence, the youngest of the Rowe sisters, never married, preferring to live with, and assist, her mother until she died. But it was Bella, the middle sister, who had the unhappiest life of all. She had married a draper from Birmingham in 1889 who subsequently did very badly in business, losing all his money along with the two hundred pounds that Thomas George Rowe had left to Bella when he died. Her husband finally found himself out of a job altogether with a growing family to support.

In 1897 things became even worse for Bella, as she became gravely ill following the birth of her youngest child. His sister's ill health worried Arthur tremendously. Not only was he fearful that she would not survive but he was worried about what would happen to the children if she died, and who would take on the responsibility and financial burden that his sister might leave behind. In a letter to Sophy, he expressed his fears:

Bella has not gone away yet after all — she is getting worse & scarcely a day without pain — sometimes it's bad all day,

Facing page: extract from a letter written by Arthur to Sophy on 17 September 1896

> *I think she will go away end of week if possible — I really don't know what will become of the children. I'm afraid it will be a bad time for all of us. I suppose it is no good worrying about it but wait and see, though I must say that at present the future seems rather complicated. Mother & Florence will want a home & all the while the former is alive they will keep the baby & what will become of the other two I can't imagine.*

After battling her illness for months Bella lost the fight for life and Florence took the children in to live with her, bringing them up as her own. Arthur gave this patched together little family a roof over their heads, as they all piled into his house in Edward Street in Southborough with him. Arthur now had the prospect of his and Sophy's family to support, as well as looking after Florence, and Bella's three young children. This end-of-terrace house by then must have felt rather crowded.

As Arthur and Sophy's forthcoming nuptials approached, the groom became anxious about the big day and quizzed Sophy on the details. He wanted to know if she intended to wear white, if there would be a large amount of people there and, most importantly for the shy and introverted artist, would he have to make a speech? If he were expected to speak at the wedding he expressed his fears, saying that he would "have a bad time of it". Later he revealed a little more of his concerns about Sophy wearing a white dress to the wedding. The problem of money was always at the back of Arthur's mind and he was naturally inclined to be thrifty in all situations. He suggested that the bride did not wear white, or cream, giving the reason that it would not "altogether suit you", although adding, "and then it would be no use afterwards". Although often sweetly romantic in his letters to his future wife, Arthur did not see the point of romance for romance's sake. Wanting desperately to secure Sophy's future, the idea of frittering away money on an expensive item of clothing that could only be worn once seemed utterly frivolous to Arthur.

Despite the artist's concerns, on this occasion at least, Sophy got her wish. Her beautiful, delicately embroidered white wedding dress, complete with an orange-blossom headdress crafted from wax, is still in the Rowe family.

Finally, with family objections overcome, in relatively good health and with a little money saved, at the age of thirty-seven

The Baptist Chapel, Bourton-on-the-Water where the couple were married in 1899

Arthur and Sophy, 1899

Arthur married thirty-year-old Sophy on 6 October 1899 at the Baptist Chapel in Bourton-on-the-Water. Not only had Sophy's father accepted his daughter's choice of husband by then but he also gave the pair his full blessing, proving this by acting as minister at the ceremony.

Sophy and Arthur headed to one of Arthur's favourite parts of the country for their honeymoon — the remote village of Sennen Cove near Land's End. Wild and windy Sennen, far from the crowds of London and the surrounding areas, was the perfect place for the quiet newly-weds to spend time together away from the pressures of work and society. In a thoughtful romantic gesture, Arthur penned a letter to his bride on their wedding day and addressed it to Sophy at their guesthouse in Sennen Cove. The letter was brief but expressive:

October 6th 99

Darling wife,

Just a line of love my own sweet wife to tell you that since yesterday morning I love you more than ever I thought it possible to love and you have made me the happiest of men — I can't imagine being happier than I am now. I thank God from the depth of my soul for the great gift he has given me and pray Him to make me worthy of you. I won't say adieu or goodbye for now I am yours always, husband & lover.

Ernesto

Chapter four

ITALY

Open my heart, and you will see
Graved inside of it, 'Italy'
Robert Browning

The beginning of Arthur's love affair with Sophy coincided with the start of a very different kind of love affair — with the country of Italy. The trip that he made to Rome on his return from Davos in April 1896 made a huge impression on Arthur. Already filled with joy and excitement after meeting his future wife, Arthur could not believe the beauty that met his eyes when he arrived in the Eternal City. He wrote these lines to Sophy expressing how he felt: "As to my first impressions of Rome they are like my last will be 'it's a town to live & die in', there is so much of interest, in fact every corner has some interest & the same can be said of the Campagna for miles round."

Arthur was inspired by the abundant art that was to be found in every corner of the country, as well as the beautiful Italian countryside. Michelangelo, Tintoretto, Titian and a host of other artists had filled almost every available space with their work, and it was these paintings and sculptures that Arthur was hungry to see during his travels, along with the remarkable architecture in cities like Rome and Florence. Arthur was immersed in the world of art when he was in Italy and he was at his most happy and contented when surrounded by art. Not only that, but the dry, warm Italian air had a positive effect on the condition of his lungs and he found that his breathing improved greatly when he was there. Arthur was pulled towards Italy during the cold winter months in England, when the air was damp and the sky was grey. His visit there in 1896 was the first of twenty-one separate trips that the artist would make to that country during the course of his life.

But Arthur did not immediately like everything about Italy. During his travels there he would stay in guesthouses or apartments, some more salubrious than others. On his first visit to Rome he was not happy about the accommodation, complaining that the ground floor bedroom that he had been given was dark and dreary and, although it had a very high (fourteen-foot) ceiling, was a "gloomy hole" overlooking a courtyard, "with the surroundings so high that I can barely see the sky".

It was not simply the accommodation that Arthur failed to become enamoured with on his premier visit to Rome. Arthur was an Englishman abroad and not everything new and different was to his taste. The Italian food, for instance, took some getting used to, as he complained,

> *I shall be glad to get back to England to get some meal that I can get my teeth through and which I can recognise. I keep asking what's this and the staple answer I get is 'a sort of roast beef' — very much sort! Or they say it's tongue — I think every Italian cow must have at least four tongues — we have it so often.*

On this first trip to Italy, Arthur visited many places to which he would return, and which he would paint later in his career. Using Rome as a base he travelled to, for instance, the ancient Roman town of Tivoli in the Sabine hills with its magnificent views of the surrounding countryside. Awed by the charm of the place,

Arthur wrote to Sophy, "it is a very ancient place & is full of interest & also the Villa D'Este is there, with its fine gardens & cypress trees, which are said to be the finest in the world, & I can quite believe it." The garden at the Villa D'Este, with its statuary and fountains, is a fine example of an Italian garden. It has been much copied over the years and now has worldwide recognition and protection, as it is included in the UNESCO World Heritage List.[14] It is little wonder that the young English artist found the place so inspirational and wanted to return again and again.

From Rome, Arthur also travelled to Frascati, a town twenty kilometres south-east of the city, in the Alban hills. The town is famous for its opulent villas and the wine of the same name that is produced in the region. Arthur immediately felt at home when he arrived there and enthusiastically wrote to Sophy, evocatively describing the new sights:

> *I arrived here (Frascati) this morning about 11 and am very pleased with my surroundings. My bedroom overlooks the Campagna — Rome lies about 15 miles to the N.W. and looks very near with the big dome of St. Peters standing out. It is dark now but as the sun was going down the Mediterranean was marked by a narrow strip of gold and it must be 20 or 25 miles away. In the foreground are villas and trees — nightingales singing all day and one at it now. We are several hundred feet above Rome, in the Alban Hills — a pleasant contrast here, to my bedroom in Rome.*

The Italian landscape was a feast for the eyes of this London born artist. Having grown up in the outskirts of that newly industrialised city with its smog and dirt and dust, to now find himself in the Alban hills looking down on the sun-drenched city of Rome, with its abundance of architectural wonders, must have given him a thrill like no other he had experienced.

There was much that impressed Arthur on his first visit, and he knew then that he would want to return many times and even talked with Sophy about buying a property on the Mediterranean island of Capri, another stopover, that he could rent out in the summer months. This dream would never become reality, but nevertheless Italy was to become Arthur's second home.

Arthur was not alone in his devotion to Italy. In recent decades the country had cast its spell on many British poets such as Robert Browning and Lord Byron, and it was by this time also a popular destination for many Victorian artists who were attracted by the romantic ideals that the country represented, as well as its history and abundant art.

Arthur was one of a group of these artists who regularly travelled around the country, stopping and painting at a number of well trodden destinations such as Capri. At the various hotels that Arthur stayed in during his Italian wanderings, he met and developed friendships with many travellers including a number of other artists.

Before long Arthur became used to the Italian way of life, began to learn the language and became immersed in the culture, even drinking the wine that often came free with every meal. He coyly admitted this to Sophy, who had strong leanings towards the temperance movement, justifying the imbibing of wine by saying it was beneficial to his health.

> *Wine is not an extra here so I drink it. I hope you don't mind? For I really think that it is good for my throat and blood — it is the ordinary wine of the island and is quite pure grape juice. I can't say I like it for I don't really like any wine or spirit but I look on it as medicinal. What does Nurse Slater say about it?*

After his initial minor reservations, Arthur embraced the Italian way of life and culture wholeheartedly. Although he had been brought up without any experience of Italy or Italians, he was open-minded and eager to learn about this new and exciting country and its people. It was not long before Arthur's distaste for the Italian "sort of roast beef" turned to enjoyment too, and he often spoke highly of Italian food, wishing that Sophy could be there to enjoy it with him.

> *We have lunch at 12.30 dinner at 6.30 — things are tasty so I eat well and don't seem to want much in between. I tried going out and getting a glass of milk in between but it is not good cows milk here — tastes like half water — all the goats have got young just now so there's no 'latte caprino' to be had but I expect there will be in a few weeks — it is good stuff to drink.*

Despite the enjoyable food, pleasant company and beautiful surroundings there was a downside to Italy, which Arthur quickly

Right: December on the Bay of Naples, 1910

A. ROWE

became aware of and which bothered him greatly. He must have witnessed poverty in the London of his childhood, but the scale of the poverty in Italy gave Arthur's heart a jolt. Being a compassionate man, the plight of some of the poorest people in the country touched him greatly, particularly in 1898 when he was staying in Bagnaia painting the ornamental parterre gardens of the Villa Lante, regarded by some as one of the most beautiful villas in Italy. The contrast between the sumptuous architectural beauty of the gardens and the desperate hand to mouth existence of the ordinary people in the villages around the area was shocking. While there he wrote to Sophy to tell her about his unsettling discoveries:

> *...after what I've heard today I almost feel that I have no right to eat what I do — the poverty in this place is beyond description...there are 4000 people in this place & now half of them are starving — year after year things go from bad to worse — crops fail — weathers bad — no work — yesterday afternoon there was a fearful thunderstorm with hailstones it did no end of damage — the people all flocked to the church crying & screaming, praying God to have mercy on them. It is a terrible state of things & there seems little hope of relief here — Italy is very poor and this is the poorest of the poor. I thank God Darling that you are not here, it would be too painful Darling to see so much misery which you could do little for.*

Despite witnessing these horrors Arthur continued to travel to Italy every winter, moving from town to town and villa to villa until the outbreak of war in 1914. He would usually have to obtain a permit to paint a particular garden or villa. These were only given to people seen as serious artists, but Arthur never had any difficulties gaining permission. He would return again and again to Naples, Florence, Rome and Ravello — a town above the Amalfi coast. The latter place was famed for its beauty, with its stunning views of the azure Mediterranean, and it is a popular destination for many artists even today. Ravello certainly held a special place in Arthur's heart, as he later gave his self-built house the same name.

In Italy, the light watercolours that Arthur was now using in his paintings of the gardens of Britain suited the subject matter perfectly. There, as at home, Arthur would paint grand villas

The Church of the Madonna Della Grazia,
Ravello, Gulf of Salerno, Italy

and their gardens, as well as scenes of the Italian countryside. Whatever Italian scene he chose to paint, there would always be a view of the far distance leading the eye into an infinite sun soaked beyond. Arthur commented on this aspect of his paintings when interviewed in 1907, explaining the importance of the "distant vista" in creating a marketable Italian painting. Arthur's paintings were invariably designed with a future sale in mind. True to this, all of his Italian paintings have a hint of the beauty that lies outside the painting — be it a snippet of the inviting blue Mediterranean from the Amalfi coast, the slumbering giant Mount Etna from Taormina in Sicily, or the mountains around Lake Como.

In a painting entitled *The Garden of the Cappuccini Monastery,* painted in 1902, the hazy turquoise Mediterranean leads the viewer's eye into the beyond of the painting. The foreground depicts the terrace of that monastery on the Amalfi coast. This terrace consists of a long passage of pillars overhung with vines. Flowers trail up the pillars and overspill from beds at the side of the passage, and the painting is bathed in sunshine. This sunny painting would have surely tempted the rich back home to visit Italy. The Cappuccini Monastery itself has succumbed to the modern-day tourist industry. No longer a sacred place of worship, it is now a hotel, and breakfast is served on the same terrace that Arthur painted over a century ago.

Many of Arthur's Italian paintings now serve as useful historical documents. His paintings depict some scenes that remain unchanged, as well as some that have disappeared for ever. Arthur was very careful to reproduce the scenes accurately, and we can be sure that any scene that he painted would faithfully represent the reality.

One scene that no longer exists is the *View of Mount Etna* from the garden of the St Domenico Palace Hotel in Taormina, Sicily. This painting, created by Arthur in 1905, shows the former monastery's stone terrace. Wisteria overhangs the terrace and a few flowering plants are scattered around the yellow stone. Mount Etna towers over the distant view and a little statue of a cherub sits on a column on the right-hand side of the painting. The peaceful scene that the painting depicts was shattered not long after Arthur put down his brush. Etna erupted in 1908, the first of many eruptions during the twentieth century[15], and during the Second World War the hotel was used as a base by the Germans and was heavily bombed by the British. The only part

The Garden of the Cappuccini Monastery, Amalfi, 1902

View of Mount Etna
from the Garden of St Domenico,
Taormina, Sicily, 1905

of the scene that has survived unscathed is the little statue, which now sits in the rebuilt monastery cloisters — now part of the hotel — a few yards from the reception area.

Arthur was not only interested in painting Italy's manicured villas and hotels but also in its faded glory. He painted several ruins including the Roman Forum, although the foreground of this painting is taken up with the purple flowers that had grown over the broken pillars and crumbling stonework.

Some of Arthur's Italian pictures depict views of nature with little interruption from man save the occasional pathway or ornate pot. One instance of this is a painting of Villa Buona Ventura (now Villa Collina) in Cadenabbia. There is no image of the villa itself in this painting. Instead there is the impressive view from the villa's gardens of Lake Como and the mountains beyond. The mountain view is carefully framed by a tree on the left of the picture, a lush border of bright pink flowers and a large ornate plant pot on an ivy-covered plinth.

Similarly a view from the garden of another of Lake Como's villas — Villa Carlotta — depicts a distant mountain. In this painting a winding path leads the eye towards the mountain while the foreground is consumed by large fir trees and rhododendrons. The mountain and the tree in the foreground reflect each other in shape and grandeur, and give the viewer a sense of the power of the nature that surrounds us even as we try to tame it in our gardens.

Some of Arthur's Italian paintings are reminiscent of the paintings of his homeland. In another painting of Villa Collina, Arthur again focussed mainly on its gardens. With its towering ordered row of fir trees, its even lawn, ornate pot in the foreground, and circular fountain, it could pass for a garden in Surrey or Kent were it not for the distant view of lake Como and the mountains beyond.

Although Arthur met with other artists and travellers from England, Russia, America and Germany while he was there, his trips to Italy were usually undertaken alone. Arthur often said that he was self-sufficient and "not dependent on company", but he did suffer from homesickness at times and often missed Sophy desperately during the months that he spent away. According to one magazine article, Arthur once wrote from Isola Bella on Lake Maggiore:

> *Here I am a solitary man in an hotel on a little island not*

Next page: Villa Carlotta, Tremezzo, Lake Como, northern Italy

200 yards long. Across the lake on the mainland I see every day about tea time a through train to Dieppe and I wish I were in it, for here at a distance of 700 or 800 miles, Dieppe seems quite near home.

It was not only Arthur who suffered during their times apart. Sophy also found it hard to cope with her husband away for long periods, although she always had company and, in contrast to her husband, was a marvellous conversationalist who could talk happily to anybody about any subject. With Arthur away she would also immerse herself in her books. An avid reader, she collected books on every subject, in particular collections of poetry, often poems with a highly religious flavour, and she would write down her favourite poems in numerous notebooks.

As the wife of an artist Sophy continually battled with financial pressures, and in January 1902 Sophy and Arthur's first child Ernest Ronald Rowe, known as Ronald, was born — increasing the pressures on them both. During this winter Arthur did not go to Italy but left home for sunnier climes on 24 March when Ronald was a mere two months old. Although Arthur was now becoming well known and respected as an artist, the family could not afford to hire any domestic help at this time, so Sophy was left alone to take care of the house and a tiny baby. Fortunately the extended family now proved its worth, as there were many relatives who would visit and ease some of the burden of the new mother.

Just eighteen months after Ronald's arrival, Sophy and Arthur's second child was born. Christabel Mary Adelaide Rowe, known as Mary (after Arthur's mother, who had died the previous year) or 'Girlie', entered their lives in July 1903. Sophy now found herself with two small children to look after almost singlehandedly, while Arthur continued to spend months away from home in pursuit of the best views. Less than two weeks after Mary's birth Arthur left home once more — this time for Scotland.

But in 1905 Arthur decided to take his family with him on his annual Italian adventure. Packing everything they would need for two young children, Arthur and Sophy left Kent for Bordighera on the Ligurian coast. Bordighera was a favourite destination for English tourists. In one period, at the end of the nineteenth century, there were as many as three thousand English guests staying in the hotels and villas of the area, compared to only two thousand local inhabitants.[16] So Sophy would have had plenty of

Previous page: Villa Buona Ventura, Cadenabbia, Lake Como, northern Italy

company while Arthur was out working, on this particular trip.

Although Arthur went to Italy for the good winter weather it was not always favourable, and from Bordighera Sophy wrote to her sister Dora, complaining:

> *I am sorry to say the bairns both have croupy coughs just now. It is these cold winds I suppose which spring up so suddenly. R has been quite unlike himself — quite subdued — but I hope they will soon be better. To-day has been very wet and they do hate a day indoors so — and I get so tired of it too as I can't sew or anything.*

With Arthur away painting, and cooped up with two young children in a hotel room, Sophy found it difficult to keep Ronald and Mary from getting into childish trouble. She explained the situation to Dora:

> *Poor mites, they have unconsciously mightily offended the Italian Major downstairs by dropping their bricks innocently out of the window on to his pate below — also on that of the servant. The last few days a lot of their bricks have mysteriously disappeared, and as I can't find them, I fear the Major has confiscated them out of revenge, and perhaps we shan't get them back. Ronald also smuggled in some stones in his coat pockets and he and Girlie dropped a few of these out of the window with the same result, so I fear we are now deemed as enemies by those below.*

The family were seldom present on Arthur's trips abroad, but Arthur never neglected to write to them. Postcards, many of them hand coloured, were sent regularly and longer letters were written whenever time permitted. Often Arthur would draw pictures for his friends and family, including some delightful sketches for his young children, many of which still survive. One letter sent to Ronald from San Remo in northern Italy in 1904, when Ronald was just thirteen months old, consists of scribbles and pictures. *(See next page.)* Ronald was too young to read, but he would have recognised the sweet little sketches of a wheelbarrow, blocks, a mouse, butter and a cat.

Italy was Arthur's first love after England, but he did travel to other countries during his career, notably France and Spain. His one visit to Spain took place in the winter of 1906–7. Again

he took Sophy with him on this trip, although on this occasion the children stayed at home with relatives. Arthur and Sophy travelled first to Seville then on to Granada. Arthur wrote to Ronald describing this alien environment and he could not find much good in the place:

> *Mother and I are now in Spain where the oranges come from and we wish that you and Mary were here with us — only there is nothing nice to eat — milk is not nice — no butter but dry bread and the jam costs ever so many pennies to buy. The chocolate is not nice and the tramcars and puff-puffs are all very dirty. Also a lot of dirty cats and dogs which have a lot of fleas…*

He added, as an afterthought, "The mosquitoes bite us every night."

Facing page: a letter written by Arthur to his son Ronald, who was too young to read at the time.
Right: Charles V Pavilion Alcazar, Seville, 1906

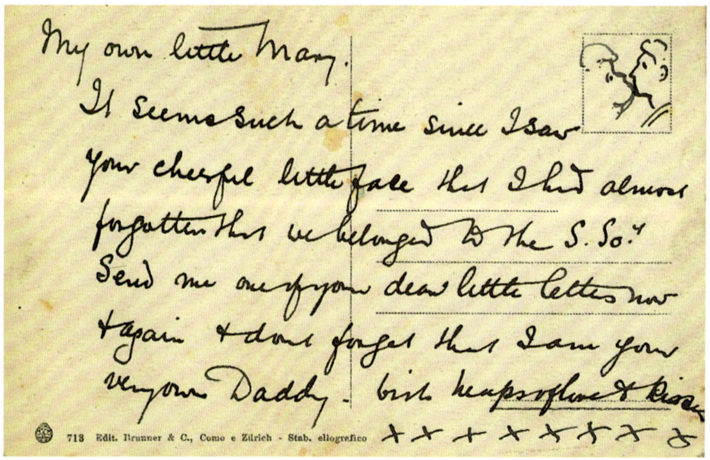

My own little Mary.
It seems such a time since I saw your cheerful little face that I had almost forgotten that we belonged to the S. So.y
Send me one of your dear little letters now & again & don't forget that I am your very own Daddy - with heaps of love & kisses
X X X X X X X X

713 Edit. Brunner & C., Como e Zürich - Stab. eliografico

This page and facing page: hand-coloured postcards sent from Arthur to Mary and Ronald

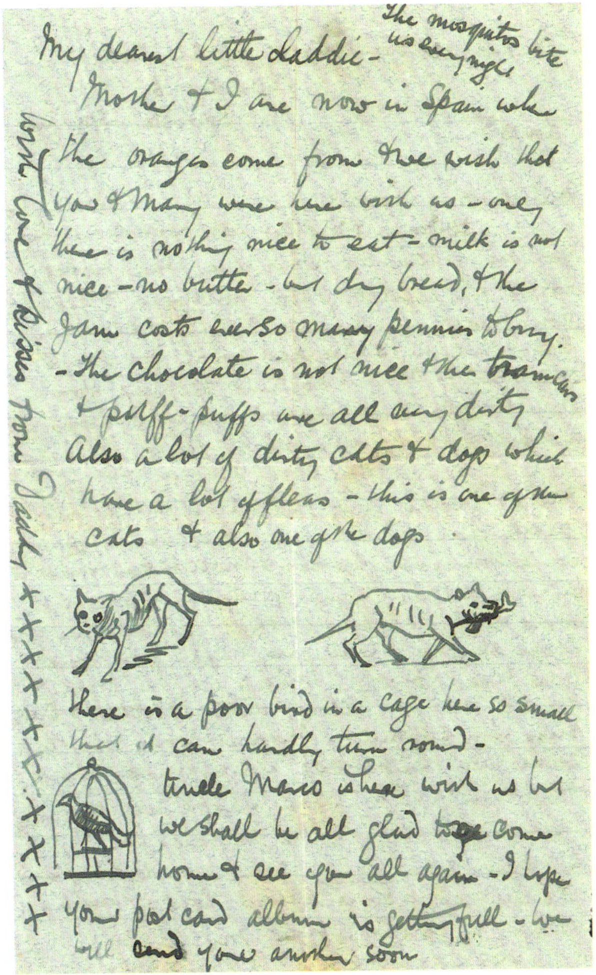

The mosquitos bite us every night

My dearest little Laddie -

Mother & I are now in Spain where the oranges come from & we wish that you & Mary were here with us - only there is nothing nice to eat - milk is not nice - no butter - but dry bread, & the jam costs ever so many pennies to buy. - The chocolate is not nice & the tramcars & puff-puffs are all very dirty also a lot of dirty cats & dogs which have a lot of fleas - this is one of the cats & also one of the dogs

There is a poor bird in a cage here so small that it can hardly turn round -

Uncle Marco is here with us but we shall be all glad to come home & see you all again - I hope your post card album is getting full - we will send you another soon

With love & kisses from Daddy xxxxxxxxxxx

Despite the difficulties, Arthur was able to paint several Spanish scenes during his stay there. *The Charles V Pavilion, Alcazar* is one example. This view of the Moorish palace in Seville again shows Arthur's delight in all things natural. The columns of the palace fade into the background along with a large palm tree. In the foreground are two fruit laden orange trees, one of which was said to be eight hundred years old according to Arthur and to have survived since the time of the Moors. Arthur depicted the view as he saw it: there are windfalls all over the ground and haphazardly left on the walls and among the potted plants.

Spain clearly did not appeal to Arthur in the same way that Italy did, as this was his one and only trip to that country. In April the following year he returned to Italy once more. The pull of the Italian landscape was great, and Arthur's heart was always at home there. Even as he lay in his bed towards the end of his life, his body wrecked by the TB that he had been battling with for years, he was still planning one last trip to his beloved second home.

Chapter five

CAREER SUCCESS

Little do ye know your own blessedness; for to travel hopefully is a better thing than to arrive, and the true success is to labor

Robert Louis Stevenson

When Arthur returned home from his first trip to Italy in June 1896, he went straight to work painting scenes from English country life. His first port of call was Greenlands, the grand home of the family of the bookseller WH Smith in Henley-on-Thames. Mr Smith, son of the late bookseller, commissioned Arthur to paint his home and gardens and paid for him to stay in a guest house in the town. Arthur was grateful to Mr Smith for his generous payments: "I am very comfortable here & so I ought to be as Mr. Smith is paying 10/- a day for me," he wrote, and Arthur did very well financially during his time there, clearing at least thirty guineas in two or three weeks. Although working hard on his paintings, Arthur was aware that it was a little too early in the year to show the garden at its finest. "The roses in the garden are lovely," he wrote to Sophy, "but not much to make a picture of as the path, background and everything is green." Ill health was a recurring theme at this time, as it was so often during Arthur's life, and he felt that he was not able to give himself completely to his work when he was unwell. Arthur later wrote that he was "quite disgusted" with the Greenlands paintings, adding, "my health has told on my work, I can see it plainly & it's rather painful to me."

But whether or not Mr Smith was happy with the paintings of his home, Arthur was learning that art buyers were a fickle bunch. Some paintings were snapped up by the owners of the gardens, others left to go into future exhibitions. In 1896 while at Greenlands, he wrote to Sophy explaining that he had recently sold a picture at the Royal Institute for twenty guineas and had offered it twice before for only ten without making a sale. The artist was coming to realise that "a picture is worth just what it will fetch", but if the right buyer saw it, he or she would pay handsomely.

It was in 1896, after he met Sophy, that Arthur began to think seriously about his future career. There was by then more at stake than ever, as there was no longer simply "ne'er do well Arthur" to consider. Financial security was now at the forefront of Arthur's mind and he wanted to make a success of his artistic endeavours for the sake of himself and his family.

Arthur understood the way the art world worked. He was aware that it was considered prestigious to belong to certain societies, and he knew that being a member of them could smooth the path ahead. But Arthur was not a showy individual and he did not care too much for these kinds of badges of honour, preferring to judge an artist by his work alone rather than his titles, as he explained to Sophy:

> *…being a member of a Royal Society carries a certain amount of standing with it and they have the right to the title of Esquire which ordinary people have not. You may always address me as Mr. if you like as I've no right to Esq. though they feel offended if addressed Mr. but all this is worth nothing.*

Despite not belonging to any of the royal societies, the young artist was beginning to have some significant success. Already, at this early stage of his career, he had had several oil paintings in the Royal Academy. Some of these paintings had been 'hung on the line' — meaning they had been displayed at eye level. The Academy chose what they considered to be the cream of the crop to be displayed on the line, so Arthur's talent was recognised and rewarded early by this influential organisation. However, he spoke about the fact that these oil paintings had not sold as the reason why he gave up this medium:

> *I used to paint in oils as much as waters but found I couldn't sell them so gave it up about 5 years ago, not entirely of course, I had my oils at Davos don't you remember…I have 5 or 6 oils now at home that have been hung at the Royal Academy some on the line but I can't sell them — shall have to give them away with a pound of tea or else as wedding presents.*

Throughout the course of his career Arthur continued to exhibit at the Royal Academy, the Royal Institute of Painters in Water Colours, and the Royal Society of British Artists, showing a variety of work. Some garden paintings were accepted such as an 1893 painting of Compton Wynyates in Warwickshire (a favourite garden of Arthur's), as well as village scenes of Clovelly and Bossington, and a watercolour with the idyllic name of *On the Banks of a Surrey Stream.* The price tags on these exhibits ranged from a modest five pounds and five shillings to over thirty pounds for a painting called *Under a Sunny Sky* of Tintagel in Cornwall.

In April 1897 Arthur held his first solo exhibition at the Golden Cross Hotel off Trafalgar Square and it was very well attended. The visitors' book still exists and lists numerous lords and ladies, including relatives of Mrs Hamlyn, along with many of Arthur's family and friends.

With a successful exhibition behind him things were going well for Arthur and he continued to build on this success, holding more exhibitions and inviting many illustrious buyers of art to view and hopefully purchase his work.

Arthur at this time had more reason than ever to work hard, paint as much as he could, achieve success and, most importantly, bring in money to support Sophy and his extended family. There was no let-up in the pace of work, as the wandering artist moved from Italy in the winter months to the gardens of England and Scotland during the spring and summer, where he painted, weather permitting, tirelessly to create a body of work

Left: On the Banks of a Surrey Stream, exhibited at the Royal Society of British Artists

that could be exhibited and hopefully sold to sustain his loved ones. Arthur was no aristocratic artist, travelling around to see the beautiful sights of Britain and Europe to feed his soul; he was a serious professional moving from one painting to the next in order to keep the pennies rolling in so that the people he loved could be fed, clothed and kept warm.

Solitude was something that Arthur was not afraid of, and he obviously derived a great deal of enjoyment from working on his own at an easel with no one but the butterflies and bees for company. But he sometimes missed the company of his family and friends, and often felt lonely and like an outsider, particularly when he found himself among a large gathering of people. For instance, during Queen Victoria's Diamond Jubilee in June 1897 Arthur was in Holnicote in Somerset painting its picturesque cottages, and wrote to Sophy about his experience: "I hope you enjoyed the Jubilee, I felt very sad and lonely that day, I saw everybody else enjoying themselves while I simply looked on as I knew no one and there was really nothing to see but I felt I must be there." The shy artist did not make friends easily and felt awkward about expressing his emotions, particularly around strangers. To find himself in the middle of this joyous crowd celebrating Victoria's sixtieth year on the throne must have been particularly difficult and unsettling. This episode underlines how Arthur's constant solo travelling must have taken its toll. It was by no means as idyllic as it might appear.

But the travelling was necessary in order for Arthur to be able to create enough pictures for the biennial solo exhibitions that were now becoming routine for him. After his initial exhibition at the Golden Cross Hotel, Arthur held exclusive exhibitions every other year. Until 1912 he showed his Italian and British paintings at the Dowdeswell and Dowdeswell Gallery in New Bond Street every two years. When this gallery closed in 1912, Arthur regularly exhibited at the Greatorex Galleries in Grafton Street. The Royal Institute of Painters in Water Colours also exhibited Arthur's paintings, twenty-one in total during the years 1886–1898, in its Piccadilly gallery. These grand exhibitions, attended by the usual aristocratic art buyers, were supplemented after 1907 with exhibitions in Arthur's own house, Ravello, in Rusthall, Kent, as well as small exhibitions in Italy. One handwritten notice for an exhibition "of a series of water colour drawings of Villa Carlotta & other gardens in Italy & England" at the Hotel Bazzoni, Tremezzo in 1912 still exists. *(See next page.)* Similarly,

the hotel itself is still there and run by the same family that was in charge in Arthur's day.

Although Dowdeswell and Dowdeswell took their cut of the profits of any painting sold at their galleries, Arthur always negotiated to secure the best deal and fought his corner over money, explaining the situation in a letter sent from Italy to Sophy in 1898:

> *...shall want an interview when I get back & see what terms they propose — they will want to make several hundred pounds of profit and expenses for certain and this child will also want several hundred & I don't quite see how we are going to do it — we shall see — I don't intend to let them have it all their own way as I have too a good connection of my own so that to a certain extent I can be independent as well as Sophy!*

Although no records exist of the financial success of his exhibitions, it is known that prices ranged from five pounds to one hundred guineas and it is estimated that he could have made as much as one thousand pounds, less the gallery commission of twenty or twenty-five per cent, at each of his biennial London sales. In addition there was income from smaller exhibitions at his home and in hotels, private commissions and book illustrations. Even when he only exhibited one or two paintings at various London galleries in the late 1890s, the prices ranged from five pounds to sixty-five guineas.

Money was never a subject that was far from the minds of both Sophy and Arthur throughout most of their lives together. Arthur was a typical Victorian in that he was extremely careful with his money. From a twenty-first century standpoint, his financial cautiousness can seem excessive. For instance, when Sophy's father died in 1912 Arthur sent his sympathies in a letter from Rome but went on to advise Sophy not to waste money on funereal dress:

> *I hardly know what to say to you in all your trouble but I do feel for you Love & wish I could put my arms around you & comfort you if ever so little…Tell me what money you must have & I must send you a cheque — don't buy more black than possible or I feel sure that you will be sorry. I don't feel that M should have an* <u>*all*</u> *black hat — white trimmed with black if you like —* R *need only have a black cloth round his arm & a black beani for Sunday.*

But this seemingly obsessive financial cautiousness was no doubt born of necessity. Although during some periods he sold many paintings for high prices, Arthur never knew when he would be incapacitated by illness and unable to work. Also the profession that he had chosen was a fragile one, and he could never accurately anticipate how many paintings he would sell a year and when, and how much money would be coming in. This was why he had to spend every penny thoughtfully and save as much as he could for the rainy day that would inevitably come.

Sophy knew that she would also have to adjust to this uncertain way of life. As the daughter of a clergyman she would have enjoyed a privileged upbringing, although probably a fairly austere one. She would not, perhaps, have been used to the constant insecurity that was the life of the artist, and struggled with the lack of funds. In a letter that she wrote to Arthur in 1906, but never sent, she tentatively asked her husband for extra money:

> *Darling you only gave me £1 for home did you know & first*

week is heavy but I expect you will send some more. And I may as well tell you I shall want some more for clothes — you see I have to set the bairns & myself up for the winter, I must get them now...

There followed a list of all the things Sophy felt she needed and the cost of each item. These included a best hat, coat, umbrella, navy silk blouse and a morning blouse for herself; winter vests and knickers for Ronald; and boots and shoes for Mary. Sophy pleaded for the money urgently before she departed for Spain, underlining the word 'now' twice to emphasise it. Obviously feeling guilty for asking, she explained her need for new clothes in this way: "I expect you'll think the list for 'self' a bit extravagant but then I am your little wife & I want to look nice & besides we will meet a lot of people & perhaps get to know some & then if I am so out of date it makes me feel self conscious."

Where Arthur never seemed to have any awareness of social standing, or at least did not care to concern himself with it, Sophy was painfully class conscious and always aware of how she would be perceived in society. The idea of wearing clothes that were "out of date" was, for her, simply unbearable. Arthur loved being an artist; it was his vocation and he never had aspirations to be anything other than a successful artist who was able to support his family. But the life of a struggling artist's wife proved to be difficult for the clergyman's daughter, who had been brought up with a good standard of living and an expectation of a certain standing within society. Although Sophy and Arthur's marriage was based on cooperation and mutual support, Sophy remained dissatisfied with the couple's position in society throughout the course of their marriage. She never truly accepted her reduced position and often worried about how she was perceived by those around her. In a letter sent from Tremezzo, northern Italy in 1921 to her daughter Mary, she talked unhappily about a couple called Allan who were staying in the same hotel as the Rowes, and who liked to spend time with all the "swell English people" who were visiting the area.

The Allans love to keep meeting them but I hate it and wish myself back in Rome or at Frascati or at home. The Allans are ever so smart on Sundays. Yesterday they were decked out for Church. I did not know them. Also in evenings they have very pretty pale blue silk dresses — "charmeuse" I think it

was called and if cold evening they wear over them pale grey silk jumpers like my grey woollen one only silk. I wish I had a silk one. Mine is too dirty to wear now — except for breakfast — and too hot. It does in bedroom.
It is cooler since the rain but has been very hot — I am always hot here — and to make me hotter D and I have a table by the door — next to the hot pipes and there I sit and stew but I dare not ask to be changed in case we are put at a table perhaps in the middle of the room. We are out of the way where we are — next to the Allans — only people have to pass us on the way out. I don't like that.

In contrast to his wife, Arthur found the whole idea of dressing up to be accepted by society as rather meaningless. He had a quiet confidence in his talent and felt that he did not need to prove himself in superficial ways like dressing correctly. In a letter from 1897 to Sophy, written from Preston Hall in Dalkeith, he talked about the subject:

I found Mr. & Mrs. Calander here with one lady visitor but they have all left this morning. Mrs. C. till Saturday or Monday and Mr. C. for longer I expect. I am left alone with the governess (French) and two or three children who have lunch with me, don't know if the 3 former will have dinner with me, I expect not — she is the daughter of a French artist who paints battle pieces. If I dine by myself, and I expect I shall, it seems absurd to dress for dinner but I suppose I must for the look of the thing. I simply hate this kind of life and feel miserably depressed…

Although his wife was dissatisfied with the family's modest lifestyle and imagined lack of respectability, Arthur did achieve a great deal of success during his career, and managed to sustain Sophy and the children and his extended family financially for many years on the back of his talent. Garden painting proved relatively lucrative and Arthur produced watercolours of the grandest gardens of Britain for the rest of his life. A 1902 painting of Dean Hole's garden in Rochester is one example. Dean Hole was founder and president of the National Rose Society, which still awards a medal named after its founder. In this painting of the influential horticulturalist's garden, like so many others by Arthur, the artist made the pathway a prominent feature of the image. The cathedral and dean's house fade into the background while the foreground is filled up with the pathway and the floral borders that spill over on to it, their blooms occupying each side of the painting in a joyous jumble of red, blue and white.

The gardens at Hampton Court Palace were the subject of a number of Arthur's paintings. Arthur found much to paint in the sixty acres of gardens at this royal palace, the gardens and state apartments of which Queen Victoria had opened to the public in 1838.[17] A large and glorious painting of the gardens, entitled *The Long Border,* painted in 1904, was shown at Arthur's 1905 exhibition. This painting is one of Arthur's larger paintings and shows again a distant building, this time Hampton Court Palace, fading into the background. Again the foreground is taken up with a pathway on the right, which draws the eye into the distance, to the palace and beyond. Next to this pathway is a strip of perfectly mown lawn. On the left hand side of the painting, and taking up by far the largest portion of the image, is a wide border of summer flowers in mixed colours, shapes and sizes, which overspill on to the smoothly mown lawn below. The painting's colours are rich, and the jewel-like red, yellow and purple flowers struggle for dominance in the scene. Arthur's excitement at recreating the image is almost tangible, and as you view it you can sense the artist's joy as he delicately added flower after flower to create this evocative image of a summer's day at the royal residence.

The eyes of a wealthy admirer soon fell on this painting and it was snapped up by this important visitor, as explained in a letter written by Sophy to her sister Dora in March of that year:

> *As far as we know his show has been very successful. The Princess of Wales came again with the Prince and he bought four more in addition to her six including the largest one of all Hampton Court, for 100 guineas so that is good isn't it.*

The Prince and Princess of Wales became King George V and Queen Mary, and this picture was later hung in Queen Mary's dining room at Marlborough House, no doubt reminding the royals and their guests of the heady days of summer as they sat through many a meal in wintertime.

The future king and queen were not the only royal patrons of Arthur's, and the gardens of Hampton Court were the scene of a memorable moment in Arthur's life and career. In the fol-

Right: Dean Hole's Garden, Rochester, 1902

lowing June, Arthur sat in the gardens under an umbrella, dressed in his usual old leggings and cape, when he became aware that there was a party of people passing behind him, and one of them stopped to watch him at work. When this happened, as it must have frequently done, Arthur had a rule that he did not look up from his work, and eventually he was aware that the viewer had moved on. A few moments later a member of the passing party came over to tell Arthur that it was Queen Alexandra herself who had stopped to watch him at work. Arthur felt that this was a tremendous honour and was even happier to learn later that the Queen had accepted the painting as a gift with a promise that she would attend Arthur's forthcoming spring exhibition.

With this royal patronage and the continual success of his exhibitions, Arthur was able to employ an architect to design the house of his dreams. His passion for Elizabethan-style timber houses had never left him and he oversaw the building of a pair of large semi-detached houses in this style in Rusthall near Tunbridge Wells in 1907. One house was sold; the other was made ready for Arthur and his little family. The house was named Ravello after one of Arthur's favourite places in Italy and was built to Arthur's specifications, including a spacious living room with plenty of light where he could display his paintings at future exhibitions. Arthur was a great collector of objects and artefacts, and he filled his home with an eclectic mixture of items that he had picked up on his travels around Britain and Europe. The cupboards were stacked with china collected in the villages that he had travelled to around England; the doors were fitted with bolts found in a lumber shop of Isola dei Pescatori, or Fisherman's Island, off Lake Maggiore; on the front door Arthur hung a bronze knocker bearing the Medici arms supported by Cupids, that he had found in an antique shop in Taormina, Sicily; and there were red tiles bordering the wainscot in the porch, which had been brought back from his recent trip to Granada in Spain.

The artist was obviously influenced by the grand gardens with which he was so familiar, as his own garden at Ravello was laid out in a formal style with an Italian influence with its arbour covered in climbing roses and strategic placing of large terracotta pots that had previously carried oil from Tuscany. He even planted a grapevine, which flourished and acted as a living reminder of his Italian travels. The garden was filled with Arthur's favourite plants, in borders, which were encouraged to blossom

Right: The Long Border, Hampton Court, 1904

E.A. Rowe

Above: Ravello, Arthur's self-built house in Rusthall, Kent. Arthur's daughter Mary is in the foreground of the picture. Left: scenes from the interior of Ravello showing some of the many objects that Arthur collected on his travels

Ravello, the artist's house in Rusthall near Tunbridge Wells, Kent. Mary is looking out of the window

and overspill from their beds to create a riot of colour in summertime in Arthur's own little Eden, as depicted in his numerous watercolours.

Although Arthur had many good years in his professional life, there had been some sadness in the lives of the family. In a letter sent by Arthur to Sophy from Sicily in December 1905, he talked about the imminent arrival of the couple's third child.

> *I hope No 3 will not come before I do. The girl ought to be sure of Dr. H's house by daylight in case she should have to go in the night — the night bell is in porch on left — day bell on right.*

Sadly the baby, a second daughter named Muriel, died when she was only one week old in March 1906. Arthur perhaps considered that the new home would mark a new beginning, a fresh start far away from the memory of the family's recent loss. It was several years before Sophy became pregnant again. The new baby, a boy named Frank Esmond Rowe — known as Esmond — was born at Ravello five years later, in March 1911, completing the family.

In addition to the commissions by garden owners and the paintings that Arthur sold at his exhibitions, he earned income from creating paintings of gardens that were then published in magazines such as *The Leisure Hour* and *Sunday at Home,* as well as in horticultural books. *The Art and Craft of Garden Making* by Thomas H Mawsom contained five colour plates of Arthur's paintings, for instance. His work also appeared in *The Studio, an Illustrated Magazine of Fine & Applied Art,* in 1903 and was reproduced on postcards. The latter were very popular at the beginning of the twentieth century. The postal service at the time was run with efficiency and precision with three posts a day. Postcards were a quick and relatively cheap way of sending messages. You could literally send a postcard to a local address in the morning, saying "See you for dinner this evening", certain that it would arrive at its destination in time. Postcards were, essentially, the email of the late Victorians. Today Arthur's paintings have not lost any of their appeal and are still frequently reproduced on postcards and greetings cards.

Some of Arthur's commissions were not just for the landowner's personal collection but had another purpose. Before the days of colour photography, coloured reproductions of certain scenes were needed for commercial reasons. For instance

Blackhurst House, Halls Hole Road, Tunbridge Wells, Kent, 1917

Sir Frank Knight — of estate agents Knight, Frank and Rutley — commissioned Arthur to paint seven views of a house called Blackhurst in Tunbridge Wells for a sales brochure. Knight wanted Arthur's images to show the house and garden in its full-coloured glory with the aim of luring prospective buyers to view the property.

The Rowe family was at last living a comfortable life in a spacious, well-equipped, modern house with Arthur, now forty-five, an established artist earning enough money to ensure that the family's standard of living was reasonably good. They even had room for a live-in servant who, to Sophy's great relief, helped out around the house and cared for the infant Esmond.

In the years after the family moved into Ravello Arthur was still away a lot, so life was not easy for Sophy with three children to look after, but from the dozens of letters that Arthur sent to the children it seems fair to deduce that his family was the centre of his world.

Arthur wrote regularly to his children expressing how much he missed them and how they were always in his thoughts, despite the miles between them. Many of the letters included drawings of things that would appeal to the children such as boats, trains and animals. To interest them Arthur would talk about the places that he was painting and would find something to say that would appeal to their young minds. For instance in 1909, when he was working at Levens Hall in Cumbria, Arthur wrote to both Mary and Ronald describing a topiary lion and included watercolour sketches of the lion to illustrate this noble leaf creature. But the letters that Arthur wrote to the two elder children were by no means always so light-hearted. Arthur often reminded them of their responsibilities to each other and to Sophy while he was away. In one letter, written from Menton near Monte Carlo to Mary in February 1908, when the little girl was just five, her father wrote: "I often wonder if you are growing into a good little woman & helping Mother all you can & whether you have left off quarrelling with brother Ronald." Arthur then added, less sternly, "I wish I could see you but I haven't forgotten you & you must not forget Dada."

In his letters, Arthur would include little sums for Ronald and Mary to tackle, as well as spellings, and he was keen that his children took their studies seriously. He also encouraged them to draw and paint, pastimes that Ronald and Mary appeared to enjoy. It was Arthur's great hope that at least one of his "bairns" would follow the family profession.

The family acquired a pet dog called Nip, later replaced with another dog, Pip, which Arthur doted on and often asked after in his letters to the children. In 1909 he wrote to Sophy about his canine companion, asking her to ensure that the children played with him sensibly:

> *...impress R. that on no account must he swing with Pippy on his lap. It is just the sort of thing he will do and he will hurt the dog seriously.*

Arthur could not always make it back for the children's birthdays, or even Christmases, but he never forgot to mention them and sent money home to Sophy for presents. On Ronald's ninth birthday in 1911, Arthur gave his son a Magic Lantern slide projector, a rather special present and an indication of how the family was doing financially at this time. Costly presents were still not purchased without a great deal of thought, but the Rowe family was by then able to indulge in life's little luxuries as Arthur's reputation and popularity grew.

As Ronald began to mature into a young man he became interested in one of his father's great passions — horticulture, and he remained a keen gardener for the rest of his life. Even when he was elderly and unsteady on his feet Ronald would stay out in the garden tending to his plants until he could literally no longer stand, and then he would lie on the grass and wait for somebody to help him up.

Years before then, when Ronald was just nine, he took charge of the garden while Arthur was away and their letters from then on contained many references to the state of it. Arthur would remind Ronald what needed to be planted and when, and which parts of the garden required weeding and pruning, sometimes using pictures to illustrate his point in a charming, light-hearted manner.

But unlike the grand gardens of the wealthy that Arthur painted, his own garden at Ravello was not planted purely for show. Arthur, with Ronald's help, grew fruit and vegetables for Sophy to prepare and cook, and which freed up some of her housekeeping budget. In 1911 Arthur wrote to Ronald from Rome saying:

> *How is your garden & mine — won't we have a grand row*

Levens 16.7.09

My dearest little Laddie

How are you getting on without Mother - being ever so good I feel sure. I have been painting a lion to day - a green one cut out of a yew tree which I daresay is 100 years old so it is quite a respectable lion it is like this:

But you have got Skip & they say that a live dog is better than a dead lion -

Goodbye I must go to bed take care of Winnie - write & tell me how Skip is - ever your loving Daddy

Letters and illustrations
sent from Arthur to Ronald and Mary
from Levens Hall in 1909

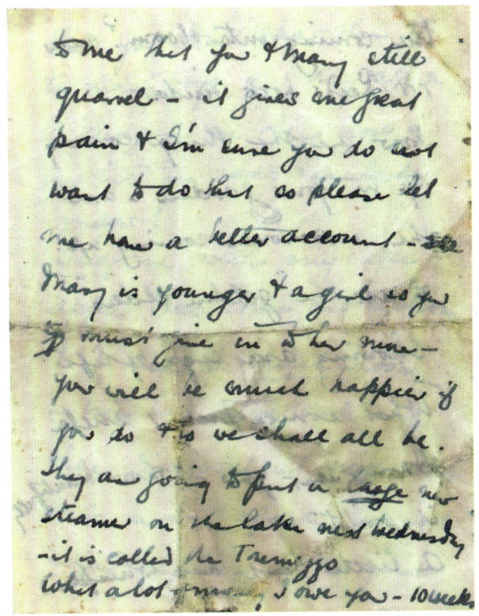

to me that you & Mary still quarrel - it gives me great pain & I'm sure you do not want to do this so please let me have a better account - Mary is younger & a girl so you must give in to her more - you will be much happier if you do & so we shall all be. They are going to put a large new steamer on the lake next Wednesday - it is called the Tremezzo What a lot [illegible] I owe you - 10 weeks

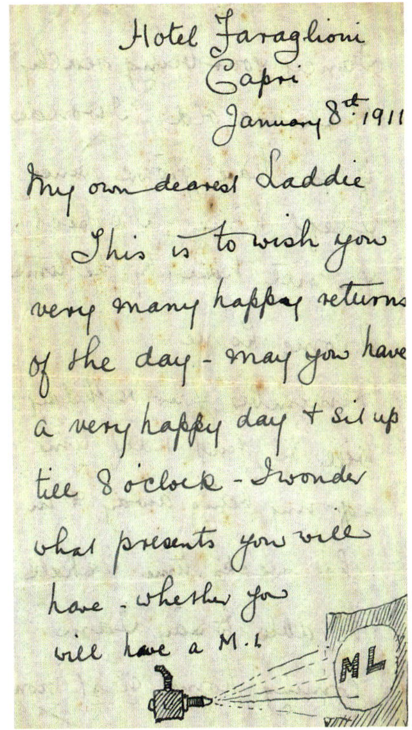

Hotel Faraglioni
Capri
January 8th 1911

My own dearest Laddie

This is to wish you very many happy returns of the day - may you have a very happy day & sit up till 8 o'clock - I wonder what presents you will have - whether you will have a M.L

Far right: a letter sent to Ronald from his father from Capri, Italy in January 1911
Above and right: extracts from a letter sent to Ronald in 1911 from Tremezzo

of cabbages between us. This year we ought to have a whole lot of strawberries.

Arthur's family was safe, secure and happy, and looking forward to a future that would be free from the uncertainty of the past, living in their comfortable, purpose-built home. Unfortunately events outside the control of Arthur, or any other ordinary man or woman in Britain, were about to have a dramatic impact on the lives of almost every person in the country and beyond.

Sophy and Arthur with Esmond, Mary, Ronald and Pip

Chapter six

A WORLD IN FLUX

life is measured by the rapidity of change, the succession of influences that modify the being

George Eliot

The Victorian era had ended with the death of the Queen on 22 January 1901 after a sixty-three year reign. Victoria's son, Edward VII, followed his mother on to the throne and the Edwardians embraced the new century with vigour. Simultaneously momentous changes were taking place in the political scene with the rise of the Labour Party and the empowerment of the working classes. Fashions came and went. Motion pictures were in their infancy along with other technological innovations such as the radio and the telephone. The world was changing at a rapid pace and the twentieth century was already making its mark on the lives of ordinary British people. The excitement that was rippling through the country would not have been lost on Arthur and his young family. But just fourteen short years after the century began, with all the hope that it brought with it, war was declared, and this was to be a war unlike any that the country had ever known.

A few months before the First World War broke out Arthur went to Italy on his usual annual visit, and he held an exhibition in May 1914 in which he exhibited over eighty paintings. But the war changed everything for the artist, whose career had been at its peak. Although his ill health prevented him from being called up to serve in the war, he was not able to work as he had been doing. With the fighting spreading across Europe, trips to his beloved Italy were now out of the question and Arthur was forced to abandon any idea of making the long journey there until the war was well and truly over. Despite the damaging effect that the English winters had on Arthur's lungs, he remained in Britain for the next few years and the damp climate made his illness progressively worse.

Arthur continued to work as much as his health would allow, but the commissions were no longer coming in as they had been. Buying art was no longer a priority for wealthy garden owners, and the gardens themselves were becoming neglected in some cases. With so many young men called up to fight there was a shortage of workers to tend the gardens and many were left to wither. Hampton Court's orangery garden, for instance, which had first been planted by William III and Mary II in the seventeenth century and had survived in some form until the early twentieth century, died away during the First World War, as there was not enough manpower to give it the required care and attention.[18]

Arthur's own garden at Ravello was now beginning to mature. Both he and Ronald continued to tend it and the whole family enjoyed the fruits of their labour. In May 1914 twelve-year-old Ronald proudly wrote these words to his father:

> *All the apple trees in our garden have either had blossom or got blossom now except the apple tree by the shed. Even the apple tree by the grape vine has had (a bit) some blossom this year for the first time. There is also a little bit of lilac out in our garden for the first time. The white broom is out in full bloom. Both of them. It looks lovely.*

As a direct result of the outbreak of war, Arthur and Sophy began to suffer financially and Arthur realised that things were only going to get worse. With three children requiring an education, all the expenses of running a large house, and money coming in only in dribs and drabs, something drastic had to be done. Arthur and Sophy realised that the reduction in their income would have to mean a scaling down of their lifestyle. In September 1915, just as the war was beginning to gather momentum, it was with great regret that Arthur and his family moved out of Ravello into a more humble house near the children's schools — 8 Belting Road in Tunbridge Wells — which they then rented for three years. Ravello had been Arthur's dream home. Every wall, window, tile and door handle had been designed by him to fit together into the perfect whole. All the objects inside and out had been collected by Arthur on his travels and chosen no doubt with the perfect spot in his house or garden in mind. Not only that but this had been the family's home. This was where Sophy, Arthur, Ronald, Mary and Esmond had lived together as a tightly knit unit, and it was where they had lived at the height of Arthur's success. To leave all this behind was devastating for Arthur and the rest of the family, and things would never be as good for the Rowe family again.

For Sophy, who had always been so class conscious, and so concerned about the family's standing in society, the move was deeply saddening. This was the second time in her life that she had suffered such a fall in her living standards, the first being when she married Arthur. Now she found herself leaving the home that had marked the family's improving status and had followed her husband's professional success. At a time when the family should have been settling down, Sophy was forced to leave the grandeur of her newly built home and move to an unremarkable Victorian terraced house. The events in Europe forced everybody to make sacrifices. Sophy did not lose any of her family in the fighting, but, because of the war, she lost her home, her comfortable life and her social standing, and this hurt her greatly.

By this time Ronald and Mary were growing into young adults, and Esmond was a lively young boy who had fallen in with a bad crowd at school and was often in trouble. Ronald, in particular, had a difficult relationship with Esmond. As his father was so often away, it was the eldest boy who was expected to act as the man of the house — tending the garden, running errands and doing odd jobs around the house, as well as helping out Arthur and Sophy's many relatives who lived nearby. Unfortunately the young man often fell short of what was expected, especially in the eyes of his father who would often write to tell him so. In one stern letter written in 1919, when Ronald was seventeen, Arthur stated that he had had enough: Ronald must do all that was expected of him or leave the family home.

> *It is very painful for me to write this but unless you behave as you should do to your mother I shall either have to make arrangements for you to live with Aunt F or else have to pay someone to take you in which you know I cannot afford. When I am away from home you ought to be all the more kind to her & helpful — you children seem to think that you must always have a good time while your Mother can slave all her life away for you. Life after all is only a preparatory school for the afterlife & as you sow now — you will reap hereafter. = There is no alternative and nothing can alter it.*

Things must have improved, as Ronald did not leave home, but his strained relationship with his brother continued to be a source of difficulty for the Rowe family. The pair just did not get along. Esmond was a bit of a tearaway who would skip school to go to the cinema, or get up to other childish mischief, and Ronald found it difficult to act both as kindly older brother and disciplinarian. Sophy found the pair's relationship trying and Arthur would do what he could from afar, offering this advice to Ronald in 1920:

> *One thing that is troubling me a great deal Ronald and that is the indifference between you and Esmond — remember he is only a little chap and has been led astray by rough boys but he is your <u>brother</u> and you must not forget it — he should look up to you and you try to help him. You need not think about that money trouble I am going to see that this is made square. You might have gone to the school and shown a little interest in him not stand aloof while there as if he did not exist. Try and meet him half way and you will feel much happier.*

The two elder children both showed signs of inheriting Arthur's artistic talent, but like him they were both introverted characters who did not thrive in company. Mary, in particular, was painfully shy, and Arthur encouraged her to make friends and socialise.

One day in 1919, a picnic had been arranged for Mary's classmates and Arthur wrote to his daughter about it, pleading with her to make an effort to get along with others:

> *I thought it was last Saturday — your picnic but I see from your letter that it is next Saturday so I do hope you will go. I want you to & will pay the bus fares — you should not be one to stand out — try to associate yourself with the girls more & you will be glad of it someday — force yourself not to sit & stand about by yourself or you will be sorry for it is that sort of thing that grows on one & becomes painful like it is with Ronald.*

Mary had a gift for portraiture. She was also an admirer of the work of Arthur's old friend Arthur Rackham and created many fantastical pictures in a similar style, including goblins, fairies and other magical creatures in her work. With her father's encouragement, she pursued her study of art and, after his death, enrolled at art school.

Despite the pressures of family life and their changing circumstances Sophy and Arthur's love remained solid, and Arthur, in particular, stayed upbeat about their life together. In 1918 he wrote to Sophy on their wedding anniversary: "Fancy that we have been married 19 years how the years have slipped by, of sunshine and shadow — really on looking back we have had more sunshine than shadow compared to other people and much to be thankful for — don't you think so?"

The war years took their toll on Arthur's income, but he still felt thankful that they had survived financially. Their drop in income had been severe, but they still had enough for the basic necessities of life. For Arthur, at least, that was enough: "Even during this war when I expected to be on my last legs I seem to have managed to rub along somehow and I think shall manage to do so through the winter if I can scrape a few more drawings together."

In the same letter, though, the extent of the family's hardship is clear, as Arthur implored Sophy to refrain from cooking the family's food — presumably in an effort to cut down on fuel costs: "When I get back couldn't we begin afresh and have no warming up even on Sundays — bread and cheese only," he penned. Arthur wrote this letter from Clovelly Court where he was staying at the invitation of his long term benefactor Christine Hamlyn, and he explained to Sophy that they were not the only ones who were having to cut back: "Even here they have one meatless day — Friday — and I think we might well have 2 a week — it would simplify matters much."

Mrs Hamlyn had helped Arthur tremendously, early in his career, with introductions to wealthy garden owners, and even when he was an established artist she still helped him professionally and personally. Arthur's wayward son, Esmond, was in need of discipline and Mrs Hamlyn unsuccessfully attempted to use her influence to secure him a place at the Bluecoat School in Horsham. Eventually Esmond went to King's Grantham at the age of ten with some financial help from the Artists' Benevolent Society.

It is likely that it was Mrs Hamlyn who introduced Arthur to Lord and Lady Lee, the owners of Chequers Court in Buckinghamshire. Arthur painted the gardens and house there in the summers of 1918 and 1919, and Lady Lee in particular was delighted with Arthur's depiction of her home. Arthur commented later that she had been, "nibbling at them [the paintings] when Lord Lee marched her off." Lord Lee invited the country's prime minister to use Chequers Court as a weekend retreat, with parliamentary approval, and gave it to the nation in October 1920. In 1921 David Lloyd George became the first prime minister occupant, and successive prime ministers have utilised the estate in the years since then.[19] A number of Arthur's paintings still hang at Chequers and must have been viewed by innumerable world leaders during the last century.

With the war coming to an end, Arthur began to think about building up his career again and started to plan another one-man exhibition at the Greatorex Galleries in London. In April 1919, forty-five of Arthur's paintings went on show there, and again the show was attended by many aristocratic art buyers keen to build up their collections. The royal family, too, had not forgotten about Arthur. Queen Alexandra and Princess Victoria attended a private view of the exhibition and each purchased a painting. In total thirty-five of the forty-five paintings were sold, making the exhibition a great success and marking another upturn in Arthur's fortunes.

Chapter seven

EVENING LIGHT

Though nothing can bring back the hour
Of splendour in the grass, of glory in the flower;
We will grieve not, rather find
Strength in what remains behind
William Wordsworth

With the war finally over Arthur speeded up the pace of his work, hoping to build on his renewed success and get his career back on track. Along with Chequers, Arthur spent a lot of time painting in Golders Hill Park, Hampstead, north London, and Hampton Court. He also travelled to Rye in Sussex, the subject of some of his early paintings, to work.

In 1920 Arthur made his first trip to Italy for six years.

Right: The North Front, Chequers Court, Buckinghamshire, 1919

Left: Golders Hill Park, Hampstead, 1919

Lake Como in the north of the country was his destination and Arthur stayed at the Hotel Regina in Lenno. Lake Como had long been a favourite place of Arthur's and he had been to the area many times before, drawn to the stunning views that included much that was good in nature: fig, pomegranate, chestnut and oleander trees grew in abundance in the area. From there he wrote to Mary about the good life that was to be had there:

> *I wish I could bring you all out here for a month or two what a fine time we could have — you would all just love it and the food too it is such a change. We have oranges and figs for dessert every day at lunch and to-day besides we had first little fried balls of white flour and mashed potatoes fried — then meat croquettes with fried squares of potato and some green vegetable then cheese and dessert.*

Arthur stayed in Italy for three months before returning home via the railways that were taking advantage of the new Simplon tunnel, which made transport between Italy and Switzerland much easier than it had ever been.

Almost as soon as he got back home, Arthur packed up his paints and easel and began his usual summer routine of work. His first destination was local — Hever Castle in Kent, childhood home of Anne Boleyn and at the time the home of Lord Astor. The gardens had only recently been laid out, between 1904 and 1908 by Joseph Cheal and Son, where previously there had been only marshland.[20] Lord Astor had commissioned Arthur to paint the gardens, which the artist duly set about doing. When he had prepared a number of paintings of the castle and its grounds, Arthur was invited to tea with Lord Astor who was interested in buying some of the paintings but wanted his wife to look over them before he made a decision. As Lady Astor was staying in Scotland at the time, Arthur was asked to take the paintings there to enable her to view them. Eventually Lord Astor purchased at least seven paintings. In a pair of the paintings of Hever that were not purchased — *Half Moon Pond* and *Vases and Peacocks* — two of Arthur's favourite subjects are prominent, namely peacocks and statuary, alongside the usual lush foliage and flowers that are almost always a major feature of his work.

In March 1921 Arthur travelled to Italy for the final time and this time Sophy travelled with her husband. By then, Arthur's health was deteriorating dramatically and he needed his wife, who

Right: Vases and Peacocks, the Italian Garden, Hever Castle, 1920

E.A.ROWE.

was also his nurse, on hand to ensure that he would be looked after should it get worse while he was there. The pair headed to Frascati near Rome to stay in the Hotel Belle Vue. Despite the success that he had enjoyed since the war, and unusually for the upbeat artist, Arthur was beginning to become pessimistic, probably as a result of his losing battle with TB. About a recent exhibition, he wrote these words to Mary: "I've heard nothing from Greatorex so am afraid the show is a failure but I won't anticipate it." Then a couple of weeks later he wrote to Mary again and his spirits had not lightened: "I have practically lost my cough and am fairly well but have not much heart to work — it seems little use producing things that won't sell — when I last heard I had only sold 10 altogether."

As Arthur's health deteriorated, so too did sales of his paintings. It seems that the taste of art collectors was changing and this was not the only thing in Britain that was in flux. Since the war the psyche of the nation had gone through a transformation. Britain had never been through such a shocking war and had never lost so many young men in such a violent way — almost a million had been killed in the fighting.[21] After the sedate late Victorian period and the hopeful excitement of the early twentieth century, the country had lost its innocence in the most brutal way imaginable. Perhaps this is why Arthur's serene paintings of British gardens no longer held their appeal. His paintings depicted a quiet, carefree Britain that was gone forever. It was perhaps too soon and too painful to be reminded of how much had been lost.

From Frascati, Arthur and Sophy travelled to Rome and from there they took the train to Tremezzo before returning home.

Despite the worsening of his health and the diminished sales of his paintings, there was little let-up in the pace of his work, as Arthur travelled to Wadhurst, Hampton Court, Bognor and Penshurst to paint in the summer of 1921.

Arthur continued to dream of Italy and began planning another visit with his old friend, the artist Alfred Moore. Arthur knew that the trip would be a strain on his health and his finances, both of which were in "such chaos that I cannot decide far ahead". Sadly Arthur never did make it back to Italy. The TB that had troubled him for so many years finally got the better of him and he died on 21 January 1922 at his house in Dorking Road, Tunbridge Wells at the age of fifty-nine. The doctor had not impressed upon the family the gravity of his condition, and neither Sophy nor the children were at his bedside when he died. *The Tunbridge Wells Courier* had these words to say in its obituary:

> *For nearly a quarter-of-a-century Mr. Rowe spent his life passing from one beautiful and famous garden to another to capture in each a vision of English loveliness and mirror it on his glowing canvas. The walled in Elizabethan garden, the hedged garden of clipped yew, the gay parterres and the wealth of flower-bordered walks all lent themselves to Mr. Rowe's facile brush, and many of his floral studies were reproduced in well-known horticultural works.*

Arthur was buried at St Peter's Parish Church in Southborough in a plot shared with his mother and later his daughter Mary.

After his death the mourning family organised a memorial exhibition of Arthur's work at the Greatorex Galleries in London, which had held so many exhibitions of Arthur's during his lifetime. Prices ranged from twelve to twenty-five guineas with the exception of one painting of Hampton Court, priced at forty-five guineas. The private view of the show was attended by the Queen, Princess Mary and Viscount Lascelles, but art collectors' appetites for garden paintings were not yet beginning to recover, and only twenty-eight of the ninety-four paintings were sold.

It would be over sixty years before Arthur was again recognised as the truly great garden painter that he was with the publication of Christopher Wood's *Painted Gardens: English Watercolours 1850–1914* and an exhibition of part of Queen Elizabeth II's collection entitled *Royal Gardens of England* held at Sandringham in 1989, which included four of Arthur's paintings.

Although forgotten for a number of years, the effect of this artist's portrayal of some of the gardens that he visited is being felt to this day. It was due to Arthur's precise rendering of the gardens that the owners of two that he painted have been able to accurately reinstate some of the gardens' original Victorian features. At Hatfield House in Hertfordshire, family seat of the Earl of Salisbury, the gardeners replanted a herbaceous border with the plants used during the Victorian era. Such was the accuracy of Arthur's work that they were able to identify the plants that were used from one of his paintings, and successfully reinstate them. At Montacute in Somerset, now owned by the National Trust, a fountain was rebuilt after the architect studied a painting of the fountain by Arthur that was hanging in the house.

Throughout his life, Arthur was always aware of the reserved nature of his character and was never inclined to drama or showiness, saying to Sophy early in their relationship that "all my life I've been so undemonstrative" and that he had "never used terms of endearment to anyone, not even my own mother". He later spoke about this in a letter to Sophy, anxious for her to be aware that, although he did not always express his emotions outwardly, they were nevertheless most definitely heartfelt.

> *You asked me to 'tell you that I loved you sometimes' and which I have never forgotten but rarely told you (directly) what you asked though I have wanted to. The fact is after telling you once I could not bring myself to keep repeating the same thing but have tried to show it in my letters. Now Darling don't think that I don't like to keep hearing you repeat it, I do, I love it, it really is nectar to me. You know darling I do love you and you are very precious to me would that I could have you now all alone to show you, so you will not mistake my reserve for want of love will you dearest one.*

The restrained expression of deeply felt emotion could also be used to describe Arthur's work. Like the artist himself the work is not brash or showy, the images it portrays are quiet and gentle, but nevertheless they are filled with a subtle warmth and humanity that is a reflection of the man behind the paintings.

Arthur was a dedicated artist with a passion for gardens in general and the formal old-world English garden in particular. He was never happier than when he was sitting on his stool on a sunny day in some fragrant garden in England, under the dappled shade of an oak tree with his easel in front of him and a sable brush in his hand. From this position, with nothing but the sound of birdsong and perhaps the gentle tinkling of a fountain for company, he would lovingly record the scene of serenity and peace. Now, although not all of us have the luxury of a sprawling old-world English garden away from the pressures and noise of modern life to enjoy, we are able to look on one of Arthur's paintings and momentarily slip into the enchanting world that is represented there, and absorb the mood of tranquillity that this artist so expertly created.

Epilogue

After Arthur's death the family remained at 41 Dorking Road, Tunbridge Wells. Ronald continued his training as an architect with London County Council staying in lodgings in a room in County Hall, Westminster during the week and returning home at weekends. Mary continued her art training in London staying in a hostel and also returning home at weekends. My father Esmond was considered too difficult for Sophy to manage and at the age of ten was packed off to boarding school. Unfortunately Mary became more and more fragile and introverted. Her mind became so disturbed that she hinted that she might take her own life. Her tutor and fellow pupils were so alarmed at her suggestions that they alerted the family and she returned home on a permanent basis, but as one or two entries in her last diary show she remained very disturbed. Without access to the sort of counselling that she would no doubt have been offered today, she took her own life on 2 June 1928, aged twenty-four.

Sophy could not bear to stay in the house after this and, with the added criticism from Arthur's sister Annie on her handling of Mary's situation, she moved into 23 Wolseley Gardens, Chiswick, London with Ronald on 28 October 1928.

Ronald became an architect for Ealing Borough Council,

so he and Sophy then moved to 20 Princess Gardens, Ealing where Sophy passed away peacefully on 7 January 1943 aged seventy-four.

Ronald remained insular and shy for the whole of his life, but in his early fifties, at his local church, he met Olwen May Thomson, a schoolteacher and lay preacher fourteen years his junior. They married in 1957 and later retired to 19 Wallace Close, Tunbridge Wells. They were together for twenty-seven years but did not have any children. Olwen now lives in a nursing home in Southampton.

Frank Esmond Rowe (the rebel) was the most successful of Arthur's children. Educated at King's Grantham for eight years he became an exceptional all round sportsman. This passion for sport continued during his career at the BBC as a radio and early television engineer. He and my mother, Eileen Mary Humphrey, married in May 1936. It was a long and happy marriage and they had three children: myself Derrick Esmond, born 1938; my brother Michael Ronald, born 1941; and our sister Barbara, born 1947. Between us we have five children and nine grandchildren. Frank Esmond died in 1992 at the age of eighty-one. Eileen Mary died in 1994 aged seventy-eight. Our sister Barbara Burley is an accomplished watercolour artist who signs her paintings Barbara Rowe.

REFERENCES

1 BBC History (www.bbc.co.uk/history/british/victorians/middle_classes_01.shtml)

2 Encyclopedia Britannica: Lambeth

3 Encyclopedia Britannica: lithography

4 Penshurst Place and Gardens (www.penshurstplace.com)

5 Hobhouse, Penelope and Wood, Christopher, *Painted Gardens: English Watercolours 1850–1914* (Pavilion Books)

6 Hitchmough, Wendy, *Arts and Crafts Gardens* (V&A Publications)

7 Royal Horticultural Society (www.rhs.org.uk/rhswebsite/documents/inner-background.pdf)

8 British History Online (www.british-history.ac.uk/report.aspx?compid=57041)

9 Helmingham Hall Gardens (www.helmingham.com)

10 Levens Hall and Gardens (www.levenshall.co.uk)

11 The New English Art Club (www.newenglishartclub.co.uk/origins_and_today.asp)

12 Exhibition Culture in London 1878–1908 database, University of Glasgow 2006 (www.exhibitionculture.arts.gla.ac.uk)

13 Encyclopedia Britannica: Robert Louis Stevenson

14 Villa d'Este (www.villadestetivoli.info/storiae.htm)

15 Encyclopedia Britannica: Mount Etna

16 Comme Di Bordighera (www.bordighera.it/international/english)

17 Historic Royal Palaces (www.hrp.org.uk/HamptonCourtPalace/sightsandstories/timelineofhamptoncourtpalace.aspx)

18 Historic Royal Palaces (www.hrp.org.uk/newsandmedia/hamptoncourtpalacelowerorangerygardenbaroqueglory.aspx)

19 Encyclopedia Britannica: Chequers

20 Hever Castle and Gardens (www.hevercastle.co.uk/Home/Gardens.aspx)

21 Encyclopedia Britannica: World War I

FURTHER READING

Browning, Robert, *The Poems of Robert Browning* (Wordsworth Poetry Library)

Eliot, George, *Felix Holt The Radical* (Penguin Classics)

Hitchmough, Wendy, *Arts and Crafts Gardens* (V&A Publications)

Hobhouse, Penelope and Wood, Christopher, *Painted Gardens: English Watercolours 1850–1914* (Pavilion Books)

Kipling, Rudyard, *The Collected Poems of Rudyard Kipling* (Wordsworth Poetry Library

Longfellow, Henry Wadsworth, *Henry Wadsworth Longfellow: Poems and Other Writings* (Library of America)

Stevenson, Robert Louis, *Virginibus Puerisque and other Papers* (Adamant Media Corporation)

Wordsworth, William, *The Collected Poems of William Wordsworth* (Wordsworth Poetry Library)

A WORD ON THE TEXT

Where extracts of letters and other documents have been reproduced in this book, the original grammar, spelling and punctuation have largely been retained.

Acknowledgments

To Alison *(The Book of My Life)* who has a wonderful way with words.

To Arthur's eldest son Ronald Rowe (January 1902–May 1984) who, it would seem, never threw anything away, leaving an archive of seven hundred letters; eight hundred postcards; his own diaries from 1916 to 1980; all the official documents including, births, deaths and marriage certificates and even EA Rowe's 1878 indenture papers; medals; and too many artefacts to list.

To my wife Pat who has helped me over the last three years to sift through it all, decipher it and type up everything thought to be informative. She has also suffered two rooms being permanently untidy and out of use, read through this book many times and put up with me.

To my sister Barbara, son Mark, and daughter Tracy for their help, advice and for contributing some of their paintings.

Finally to the late Mr Christopher Wood for his past research on EA Rowe and for permission to quote from his book *Painted Gardens.*